QUICK AND EASY VIETNAMESE

Published in 2024 by Hardie Grant Books,
an imprint of Hardie Grant Publishing

Hardie Grant Books (London)
5th & 6th Floors
52–54 Southwark Street
London SE1 1UN

Hardie Grant Books (Melbourne)
Building 1, 658 Church Street
Richmond, Victoria 3121

hardiegrantbooks.com

British Library Cataloguing-in-Publication Data.
A catalogue record for this book is available from the British Library.

Quick and Easy Vietnamese
ISBN: 978-1-78488-699-8

10 9 8 7 6 5 4 3 2 1

Publishing Director: Kajal Mistry
Senior Editor: Eila Purvis
Design and Art Direction: Evi-O.Studio | Susan Le
Typesetting: Evi-O.Studio | Doreen Zheng
Illustrations: Evi-O.Studio | Siena Zadro
Photographer: Uyen Luu
Photography assistant: Laurie Noble
Copy-editor: Lucy Kingett
Proofreader: Kathy Steer
Food Stylist: Lucy Turnball
Food stylist assistants: Immy Mucklow and Freya Matchett
Prop Stylist: Hannah Wilkinson
Indexer: Cathy Heath
Production Controller: Sabeena Atchia

Colour reproduction by p2d
Printed and bound in China
by Leo Paper Products Ltd.

FSC
www.fsc.org
MIX
Paper | Supporting responsible forestry
FSC™ C020056

QUICK & EASY VIETNAMESE

Everyday Vietnamese
Recipes for the Home Cook

Uyen Luu

Hardie Grant
BOOKS

INTRODUCTION

Growing up, I didn't hang around the kitchen, tailing my mum and watching her every move. In fact, she didn't teach me how to cook at all, and instead would often tell me to get out and go and do my homework. It wasn't until I needed to cook for myself and began to take great interest in it that my mother helped me to learn the traditional ways of cooking Vietnamese dishes, giving me the tools I needed to create my own modern versions. Now, I am a my mother, I am pleased to be giving my daughter the skills she needs like my mother gave me. I feel that I have inherited my mum's kitchen mannerisms, too.

My mum didn't know how to cook when she arrived in the UK after the Vietnam war as a refugee. I was five years old and my little brother was just three. Her need to feed us, as well as her love of eating, prompted her to learn and over time, she evolved be to the best cook I know. Memories of her cooking in my kitchen are etched in my mind. I remember her moving about with a mixture of vigour and grace from one pot to another, tasting and adjusting. She fetched from the refrigerator (which she saved up for six months to buy), she washed, rinsed, drained and chopped. Her north-facing window was full of herb and spring onion (scallion) cuttings in old jars. Her pantry was a mess of half-eaten 20 kg (44 lb) bags of jasmine, sticky and broken rice, boxes of instant ramen (because it's cheaper to buy them this way), rice noodles falling out of their packets and a disarray of opened and then elasticated packets of spices, chicken powder and stock cubes. Opened bottles of rice wine vinegar left sticky rings everywhere, and everything was dusted with the fine white powder of rice flour and finished with a few scatterings of peppercorns in between.

During the half-term breaks from school and in the summer holidays, I would often tidy the kitchen for her, buying plywood storage drawers from IKEA for her loose things, removing old wall paper from the distant past, repainting walls and even retiling the kitchen splashback. I had no idea what I was doing other than from the advice given to me by handymen at local hardware shops but she let me do it and I learnt how to DIY. I laid the kitchen laminate flooring on my twelfth Christmas with the rice cooker whistling its hot air in the background and I blindly baked cakes without recipes (Google didn't exist then) at the weekends. I learnt from my mistakes and got better, and so did she. Over time, things became quick and easy.

I still fantasise about cooking with my grandmothers, remembering *bà nội* (my dad's mum) tending to a beautiful lemongrass broth in the early morning Sài Gòn light and *bà ngoại* (my mum's mum) stirring a star anise-scented stew under the fluorescent light in her backyard in Phan Thiết, with the hum of cicadas hiding inside a green abandoned war tank as background music. Though they didn't know each other, but there were certain habits they shared. They would throw baguettes into green woven pandan baskets, tearing them apart, crumbs falling, and slathering La Vache Qui Rit (Laughing Cow) cheese on the fluffy middles. Bà nội would shake off a bouquet of dripping wet Thai basil stems, droplets falling over my head to cool me down. I can still hear her soft, high-pitched giggle and songs. They would slice lime quarters with small, blunt knives and bash garlic, chilli, lime and sugar together with fish sauce to make delicious dipping sauces. I remember bearded prawns (shrimp) lined up inside wobbly old metal steamers, the steam from simmering coconut water cloudy against the bright sun. They fed me sweet, fleshy white coconut meat, scraped with a long dessert spoon from young green shells. Everything seemed calm and easy.

I wish I had learned more from them – I never saw my bà ngoại again after the exodus that followed the war. My other grandmother emigrated to Little Saigon in Orange County, California, where the climate was parallel to Vietnam. She lived with my grandfather in a quiet, suburban trailer park. It was huge, clean and tidy. In her American-sized kitchen, she showed me the secrets to her lemongrass noodle soup (bún bò Huế). The broth was covered in pools of bubbling annatto oil, which shimmered under the tungsten glow of the overhead lights.

Bà nội knew how to cook for an occasion. Back in Sài Gòn, to make ends meet after the communist takeover, she used to set up makeshift pop-up stalls out of our living room on August Revolution Street every morning. She would sell bún bò Huế next to parked Hondas and fold-up tables. Once in California, she would still cook Vietnamese feasts in her kitchen when the family got together, such as for my grandparents' 50th wedding anniversary – it was a big cause for celebration. In the busy kitchen was a pot of simmering broth and bones. The worktop was covered with all the toppings of the famous Huế speciality, from perilla leaves, banana blossom and steamed Huế sausages wrapped in banana leaves to sliced ham hock

and tender beef short rib slices. For those all-important while-you-wait-for-the-broth-to-cook snacks, there was an array of steaming sea snails, clams, lobster and crayfish attended to by my uncles. The family poured beer into dimpled pint glasses filled with ice cubes – 'một, hai, ba, dô!' (one, two, three, in, meaning cheers). We picked and dipped the seafood in fish sauce, chilli, black pepper and lime juice. The crabs, freshly caught at the local beach earlier that morning, were cracked open with a nutcracker; their long, hairy legs filled with the sweetest, juiciest shards of flesh.

Suddenly, my uncle, chú Hiển, said he felt like eating shaking beef. While we chatted, snacked and sat around together, he brought over a small chopping board. Totally unflustered, he slapped a big piece of steak onto the board and sliced it into cubes at the table, whistling as he went. He marinated and seasoned it without fuss and then quietly walked off to shake it in a hot pan over the barbecue for a couple of minutes. With no bother, another plate of food was made for everyone to enjoy together, along with a salad of herbs and colourful lettuces lightly dressed in vinegar, sugar and black pepper. Cooking and feasting hand in hand.

From my grandmother's relaxed and peaceful composure, I saw how much she enjoyed and thrived among all the little jobs of prepping this or that to create a bowlful of joy. The true essence of her homeland and her family was there in her kitchen that day. Perhaps this is the Vietnamese way – a kind of organised and calm chaos, letting things be and working around everything that is near you, by you or imposed on you with a great sense of tranquility. Much like the Sài Gòn traffic.

When the noodle soup was ready, we all gathered around a large table. My aunties brought the platters of herbs and plates of limes, chillies and dipping sauces to the table. My grandmother made final adjustments to the broth. We ate almost in silence, because such a beautiful broth demands your full attention. Every bite was a thing of art and beauty, full of textures, opposites and flavour. It was an expression of all that she was and all that she gave. It was filled with love.

These dining moments have shaped my whole life. I want to eat well every day, whether I am ultra-busy or roaming around with plenty of free time. I love a good meal – who doesn't? It's important to me. It serves me mentally and physically.

To me, eating well equals a happier life.

My family have always demonstrated how easy cooking is. But more than that, how enjoyable the task at hand is. They relish the act of cooking and make it feel so effortless, and I have adopted their ways – I always demand a calm, easy kitchen. There is nothing better than cooking a good meal and seeing people enjoy it – and I want to show you just how quick and easy it can be.

I can't help it! I am a feeder, constantly having the desire to cook and feed. I love creating feasts midweek, weekends or special occasions, giving it my all. There is a gut feeling of wanting and needing to feed brewing deep from inside, bred into me from long lines of blood ancestry who also love to feed or found it their job to do so. It is me saying, hey, I love you or I like you guys! Eat some nice things that I have made. Or it is also saying, this is me, I am good just like my food is. I hope for your approval. Our relationship to food stems so much with how we have grown up and how we have layered ourselves with sheets of history, flavoured in many ways. I am addicted to the highs and intoxicating adrenaline of cooking for many at my supper clubs and dinner parties, devoted to making the best Vietnamese food that I can. At home, I am equally excited about cooking for my family and letting them into the joys of comfort as well as any new-found techniques, fascinating seasonal ingredients and seeing the enjoyment of my meals being chewed and swallowed up, a symbol of loved ones taking in all that I am and all that I give to them.

HOW I COOK AT HOME

I learned how to cook because I enjoy cooking and I keep at it. But don't get me wrong – I don't cook every day. I can be the laziest cook, as my work revolves around food. Sometimes I am happy to go without cooking for days on end and let someone else do it instead. I love it when other people cook for me! When I do cook, I do it because it relaxes me. I cook for pleasure; this way, my food often tastes good. If I don't have time, I'll muster up something simple like a plate of noodles, using a handful of ingredients or a dish that I can just throw into one pan and switch on the rice cooker. I often thank myself for the extra curry I made and froze for future occasions.

That doesn't mean I always want to spend hours in the kitchen, though. When I am cooking at home, I cut corners, gather and substitute ingredients. In this book, I will share the tips and hacks I use daily in my kitchen to get meals on tables. Slicing, chopping and cooking should be simple and fuss-free.

The more I cooked, the more I learnt about timings, seasoning and the behaviour of ingredients when using different cooking methods. I want to add as many plants as I can to a recipe, making sure we consume at least 30 a week, in all colours of the rainbow. Sometimes I manage to include up to 12 plants in one meal – it is a game I play with myself, to try and include as many as possible with each meal.

My shop for the week has become a lot smaller. We try to reduce the amount of ultra-processed foods, like ready-meals and desserts, without infringing on too many delights. I still love the odd comfort foods like cheese slices, tinned ravioli and custard as a treat. I do buy from my favourite supermarkets, but I don't buy everything from there. I like a handful of proteins and what's good value. I choose to purchase all my fruit and veg at a local greengrocers and supplies at an Asian grocery. Often stocking up the freezer with ready-made dumplings. I visit the fishmonger and butcher for feasts and special occasions – and I tend to use the produce on the same day I purchase them. I have stopped succumbing to the notion that everything can be purchased in one superstore – it doesn't really save on time, I don't get the quality and taste I want and I don't want to support one giant corporation.

Through writing my books, I have since discovered so many things that I love to make at home because they are so quick and easy for me to prepare. These include yoghurt, thick-cut noodles, pasta, soya milk, kimchi and so on. Like a true Vietnamese, I love eating plants, and this features heavily in my cooking.

Sometimes my heart is all in it, sometimes I just want something simple to eat but still need everything to taste good and be good for you.

MY TOP TIPS

Know your cupboard staples

I use stock cubes, pastes and powders and often buy other ingredients that are ready-made. I don't always have time to make everything from scratch and I want to make life easy. Keeping a good stock of storecupboard ingredients also means it's easy to throw together a meal without going shopping. Recognise the taste of the condiments so you know how much to use and if they bring the desired flavours to your cooking. For example, different brands of soy sauces will taste different, some saltier than others.

Preparation is key

Chop or slice everything you need, starting with shallots, onions, garlic and vegetables, then prepare any meat or fish afterwards – that way, you just use one chopping board. Less washing up!

Organise your work surface

Put things to chop on one side, a plate or board for chopped things on the other side and have a bowl for scraps for the compost bin. Create a place to put ingredients that need to go back in the refrigerator or cupboard.

Keep your eye on the clock

If you need to fry shallots, onions or aromatics like lemongrass, ginger and garlic, then get them going while you chop everything else. Don't overcook or undercook. In Vietnamese cooking, things are done quickly.

Be present

You should be at one with the pan and your chopping board (I know it's a cliché, but it's true). Concentrating and pouring a little dedication into your cooking yields good results even if you cheat.

Trust your palate and always taste your cooking as you go

You are the master of your cooking. You may prefer things to be more sour or sweeter, so go for it and make a good balance for yourself.

Enjoy yourself!

I love listening to a good audiobook, an interesting radio talk show or to music when cooking. Remember that the more you prep and cook when time permits, the easier and quicker cooking becomes during the week. Massage the cabbage for a kimchi, sink your hands in noodle dough and don't forget to make the desserts, cake, waffles and yoghurts for the week.

A NOTE ON RECIPES

So much of the Vietnamese way of cooking is a bit of this and a bit of that, adding a splash here and a pinch there. Sometimes they measure things with rice bowls or coffee and soup spoons. I have written the recipes more precisely so that they match my preferred balance of flavours and replicate how things taste when I cook at home. However, sometimes I will suggest a range of weights, for example 100–200 g (3½–7 oz) of salmon. This means you can choose how much or how little you would like to include based on what you prefer or have to hand. It doesn't matter that much to the overall flavour of the dish.

While writing the recipes I also kept in mind the accessibility of ingredients. Everything you need should be available at your local small supermarket, independent greengrocer, fishmonger, butcher and Asian supermarket.

For dipping sauces, I tend to use maple syrup as the sweetness, but anything sweet and syrupy would work. You could use caster (superfine) sugar, honey, agave nectar, coconut syrup, or even marmalade.

Most of the dipping sauces/dressings in the book can be made using storecupboard ingredients, too. If you can get hold of ready-made sauces and prefer to use these, though, go for it. I have nothing against using the odd jar or cube of something on those lazy/too tired/can't be bothered to cook evenings. Even if I make my own broth, I still add a stock cube for extra umami depth. If you can get hold of *phở* stock cubes or ready-made pastes, do use them, just jazz them up with garlic, shallots and fresh vegetables and herbs.

A little MSG is great to add oomph to many dishes. It is great to round off a broth with ½ teaspoon or so. I use flavour enhancers like commercial mushroom, chicken or pork seasoning powder, which most likely contain MSG. Sodium glutamate is naturally occurring in many common foods and fresh produce. Research and source the ones you find comfortable using, preferably without palm oil.

Although I have included recipes for homemade noodles (pages 212 and 214), yoghurt (page 188) and kimchi (pages 207), I also buy these as I am not going to make everything from scratch every time. These recipes are for when you can't get hold of them easily in the shops or if you find it rewarding to make your own on a spare afternoon.

Optional options

Sometimes the recipes include optional ingredients. It's always good to use these if they are available, but don't feel the need to go out of your way and definitely don't let the fact you don't have one ingredient stop you from making something.

I will always say that chillies and chilli sauce are optional because I am conscious of young children sharing meals – they are always welcome to enjoy everything at the Vietnamese table. How hot you like your food depends on you, so go for it or don't. You can deseed or keep the seeds in your chillies when cooking – it's up to you. My chilli tolerance is good, but I don't like things to be too spicy because I want everything to be balanced and I love to taste the overall flavours of a dish.

Substitutions

If you don't have a certain vegetable or herb, feel free to choose something else. This also applies to noodles – I have suggested what I believe to be the best-shaped noodles for each recipe based on how they work with the rest of the ingredients, but don't let that stop you if you don't have the right ones. Use what you already have before buying something else.

Fish sauce

Fish sauce is made from fermented anchovies and is the staple of Vietnamese cuisine. It is usually used instead of salt to season and flavour dishes. In fact, I often use fish sauce in my Italian cooking at home, as it is similar to garum (a Roman fermented fish sauce that has seen a recent resurgence in the culinary scene). Premium fish sauce is fermented for a long amount of time (around 18–24 months) in clay vats or wooden barrels so that it has the time and climate it needs to mature properly. Lower-grade fish sauce is fermented for 6 months and is usually diluted, meaning there is less flavour but more odour.

Try to use the best-quality fish sauce you can. It will make a huge difference to any cooking you do. You will automatically upgrade to being the best cook ever if you use a premium fish sauce! I recommend the Three Crabs or Red Boat brands if you can get them. One large bottle usually lasts a few months in my household and there is no need to worry about it taking up space in the refrigerator it as it can happily be stored at room temperature.

THINGS I NEED IN MY VIETNAMESE KITCHEN

I do own quite a variety of cooking utensils, but judging from my daily dishwasher loads, I have come to the conclusion that I only ever use the most basic items. As with most typical, humble Vietnamese kitchens that need to maximise space, only modest and simplistic equipment is needed to make some of the most flavoursome and beautiful meals. The recipes in this book do not call for anything a good knife cannot do.

Cooking essentials

1. A good, sharp and reliable chef's knife and a serrated knife
2. Sharp kitchen scissors
3. A carbon-steel wok, gently seasoned at first and then wiped down after every wash with a touch of oil on paper towels
4. A large bamboo steamer or a metal steaming basket that fits on or inside a large frying pan with a lid
5. Four different-sized pots with lids, from small to large
6. Baking dishes, roasting tins and baking sheets for the oven
7. A lidded casserole dish (Dutch oven)
8. Cooking chopsticks, spatulas and metal tongs
9. Basic utensils like a peeler, zester, julienne grater and rolling pin
10. A basic rice cooker with cook and keep warm functions

Small appliances
(that are nice to have but not a deal-breaker)

1. An instant pot with slow, pressure and rice cooker functions
2. A hand-held blender or mini chopper
3. A waffle machine
4. An electric grill/sandwich maker
5. A microwave
6. A food processor
7. A stand mixer with pasta attachment

THINGS IN MY PANTRY

1. Noodles and rice: a supply of various noodles, jasmine and/or basmati rice
2. Premium quality sauces: fish sauce, soy sauce, oyster and vegetarian oyster sauce
3. Good quality vinegars: mirin, cider vinegar, rice wine vinegar, onion vinegar
4. Sweeteners: maple syrup, honey, date or pomegranate molasses, palm sugar, rock sugar, caster (superfine) sugar
5. Oils: extra virgin olive oil, rapeseed oil, vegetable oil
6. Chilli: crispy chilli oil, chilli sauce, flakes, powder
7. Fresh pantry: small round shallots, onion, garlic, ginger, eggs
8. Tins: sardines, mackerel, sweetcorn, coconut milk, condensed milk
9. Dry ingredients: rice, tapioca and plain (all-purpose) flour, cornflour, baking powder, agar flakes, tapioca pearls

NƯỚC MẮM NHĨ
THREE CRABS Brand
FISH SAUCE
순멸치액젓 삼게상표
Net 682ml 24 Fl. Oz (1 Pt. 4 Fl. Oz)
SAVOY
vegetable umami

HOW I COOK FAMILY-STYLE DINNERS

There is a Vietnamese way to cook (similar among all South East Asians) wherein the time to cook is productively spent. Cooking time is spent making many dishes. The Vietnamese way is to be active and resourceful with whatever you have, maximising flavour and ingredients and never wasting a thing, not even time. This attitude can be applied to everyday 'rice' dinners where the family sit together and share an array of quick and easy dishes with rice.

Bring out leftovers. Always have a supply of shop-bought or homemade kimchi (or other ferments) – one homemade jar usually lasts a 2–4 weeks. Flash cook a couple of vegetable-based dishes: a quick 5 minute stir-fry and a quick soup, preparing them side-by-side at the same time. While a fish is frying or braising make a simple dipping sauce. Put done things out on the table and continue with the rest, and before you know it, there is a mid-week feast.

USING ALL THE SPACE IN THE OVEN

If I have time as I'm making something that will be cooked in the oven, I usually also have plans for baking potatoes (an easy microwaveable lunch the next day). I usually prepare for a clay pot of fish to braise in coconut water and palm sugar or a curry. Sometimes I slice up sweet potatoes or celeriac (celery root) into batons to go in the oven, and to then be used for future meals. It feels productive and saves energy by making use of the shared heat and space. Make use of the oven heat (after use) to cultivate a batch of yoghurt. Most importantly, however, it saves me time in the near future because I can simply heat those things up. I love my microwave for things like that.

MAKING USE OF THE HOB

While the tofu is gently browning or a braised pot is simmering away make a quick soup for the table! I usually have chicken stock in the refrigerator or freezer, but if not, I use a chicken or vegetable stock cube. Heat it up with a knob of sliced ginger, season, then once it comes to the boil, remove it from the heat and let it infuse. Wash some vegetables and have them ready in a colander – watercress, thinly sliced winter melon, Chinese mustard greens or spinach are all good. They will go into the broth at the end for a couple of minutes, then the soup can be poured into a large sharing bowl for everyone to help themselves to. When boiling water or making broth, keep a lid on the pan and turn the heat down to conserve energy. Remember that you can cook with the residual heat if you keep a lid on.

THE FINISHING TOUCHES

While the main dishes are frying, braising, steaming or baking, I have time to prepare the vegetables and stir-fry, so that everything is ready to go when the time is right. Make the all-important delicious dressing or dipping sauce. Set the table, wash up and start on a quick dessert, like sliced fruit salad, jelly (jello) or even cake.

WEEKEND PREP

When cooking at the weekend, use the time to prepare for the week. Make a little more of whatever you're making to have for lunch the next day. Make extra sauces or dressings and keep them in a little jar in the refrigerator for another meal during the week. Make basics like noodles, broths, soya milk and kimchi or a batch of dessert to enjoy. Easy prep like peeling a container of shallots and garlic really helps with midweek cooking.

FAMILY STYLE

Choose one from each of the sections below to make a lovely midweek and/or weekend sharing rice meal. For the recipes marked with an asterisk, you can make the most of the oven space and cook another dish at the same time to eat tomorrow (for example a braising dish that can simply go in the oven with a few baked potatoes and roasted vegetables). You'll thank yourself. These can simply be reheated during the week, making your evening meals quick and easy.

Plain rice PAGE 200
or egg fried rice PAGE 203

A vegetable stir-fry and/or salad

Leafy Orange and Ginger Salad with Marinated Artichokes PAGE 54
Stir-fried Kohlrabi with Chopped Prawns and Chives PAGE 59
Sweet and Sour Crispy Tofu with Green Beans PAGE 65
Garlicky Greens with Fermented Tofu PAGE 69

A sharing soup

Kimchi, Tofu and Tomato Egg Drop Soup PAGE 92
Winter Melon Soup with Coriander PAGE 95
Watercress Soup with Fish Balls PAGE 18
Sunshine Salmon, Tomato, Pineapple and Dill Soup PAGE 90

A protein dish

Lemony Ginger Pork Belly with Chinese Cabbage* PAGE 124
Quick-braised Salmon Steaks with Palm Sugar and Fish Sauce PAGE 132
Baked Sea Bass with Leeks, Lemon and Samphire PAGE 134
Dill Fishcakes PAGE 136
Pan-fried Fish with Green Mango PAGE 138
Sliced Pork Chop with Kimchi and Lemongrass PAGE 126
Steamed Egg Terrine* PAGE 41
Rice-cooker Chicken and Rice PAGE 129

...or something that doesn't need a vegetable side or a soup as it's full of veg already

Chicken and Cauliflower Coconut Curry PAGE 130
Lemongrass and Star Anise Chicken Stew or Pie* PAGE 159
Any noodle dish PAGES 100–118

A quick dessert

Pandan Mochi Waffles PAGE 172
Banana Fritters PAGE 176
Tofu Pudding with Ginger Syrup PAGE 181
Berries and Cherries and Coconut Cake* PAGE 187
Sweetcorn Rice Pudding PAGE 184

ONE CHICKEN, FOUR MEALS

If you are a small family or just two people, one large free-range, corn-fed chicken can be used to make the following four out of five very delicious meals:

- Chicken Noodle Soup with Omelette Strips and Fried Shallots PAGE 83
  with half the chicken.
- Chicken Salad and Mushroom Rice PAGE 52
  with leftovers from the soup.
- Rice-cooker Chicken and Rice PAGE 129
  or Chicken and Cauliflower Coconut Curry PAGE 130
  with the other half of the chicken.
- Get-well-soon Chicken Rice Porridge PAGE 84
  with the gizzards and any trimmings, plus leftover broth.

Ask your butcher to halve the chicken for you or do it yourself by spatchcocking it first. To do this, use a pair of kitchen scissors to cut down the length of the chicken's spine. Turn it over and squash the bird at the breast with your palm so that it lies flat. Then, use the scissors to cut down the length of the breast. Reserve half in a clean airtight box and use within a few days.

Chicken tips

Although you can use a roasted chicken carcass to make stock, the best and most pure broth comes from simmering a raw free-range, corn-fed chicken. Purchase legs or thighs and wings for a quick and easy broth, then season with a stock cube, fish sauce and perhaps some ginger or lemongrass.

To give broth more oomph, I like to add a teaspoon of mushroom seasoning, a chicken stock cube or chicken powder. A little MSG can be used, too.

For noodle soups, chicken that is sliced gives the entire dish more volume and bite. Although it is OK to use torn chicken, the texture won't be as good. Torn chicken is great in salads.

Shop-bought chicken, pre-cooked in a communal rotisserie is great if you want to top up some broth or rice porridge with protein or use throughout the week in a few recipes, which cuts out the cooking time.

There are various price ranges in chicken. I tend to avoid the cheap and the expensive ones but will pay extra for the free-range, yellow, corn-fed ones.

HOW TO REDUCE WASTE (AND SAVE MONEY) IN THE KITCHEN

The Vietnamese method of cooking maximises ingredients and reduces wastage. Every part of the fruit, vegetable or animal is used to make something delicious. Here are some of the habits and techniques I practise in my kitchen.

HERBS

Unless they are tough and inedible, the stems and stalks of herbs and vegetables should be used – never throw away stalks of coriander (cilantro), as they have great flavour and texture. They can be sliced up thinly to go into sauces or to be sprinkled over finished dishes.

If you have a lot of leftover herbs lying around, make a pesto with them, dehydrate them, finely chop them and combine them with butter or use them up in stir-fries and broths.

To keep fresh

When you can – preferably straightaway after shopping – wash your herbs and then submerge them in clean, cold water for 30 minutes–1 hour. Use a salad spinner to dry the leaves, then store in an airtight container in the refrigerator. Some herbs, such as perilla and Vietnamese lemon balm and coriander (cilantro) can last up to 3 weeks like this, some a week. Make sure you separate different herbs in the box with paper towels (or different compartments if possible) if they are sharing the space as some tend to wilt faster than others and you don't want to ruin the whole lot.

The exceptions to this method are Thai basil and garlic chives, which I tend not to wash until I need them, instead keeping them in their separate bags. Thai basil oxidises and bruises easily and garlic chives can give off a deadly stink if they sit in moisture for too long.

To cook

Herbs are not only used as a garnish in Vietnamese cooking – they are thought of as vegetables in their own right. Treat them as tasty elements in your cooking and throw lots of coriander (cilantro) or other herbs into your stir-fries or noodles, then garnish with some fresh leaves as well.

To preserve

I love making a pesto from all different sorts of herbs. It's great to spread on bread as a quick snack or to smother on pasta or noodles. Use the coriander pesto recipe on page 47 as a reference, replacing the coriander (cilantro) with your chosen herb. When storing it in a jar, make sure you have a good plug of oil on top to submerge the paste. This means it will keep longer, stopping it from going mouldy in the refrigerator.

To dehydrate

It's easy to dehydrate your own herbs at home. Spread them out on a baking sheet and dry in a 70°C fan (195°F) oven for 25–30 minutes – the house will smell amazing! When cool enough, crush the leaves with your fingers, then crush them further in a mortar and pestle. You can also run the powder through a sieve (fine mesh strainer) to remove any stalks and spines in the leaves. Mix the herb powder with sea salt in a 1:5 ratio then store in a clean jar for use in your cooking – you could even by add lime or lemon zest later on. This is great to sprinkle on plain or sticky rice.

The same technique works well with sugar, which is a great addition to a fruit salad or a dressing – add it to fish sauce to make a delicious dressing for fried fish.

Re-rooting

Herbs with hardy, thicker stalks such as Vietnamese coriander (cilantro), Thai basil, Vietnamese lemon balm, perilla and mint can be re-rooted very easily by placing them in a jar of water on a windowsill. In a week, streams of roots will appear, which means they are ready to be planted. Or, simply keep the jars on the windowsill and use the new leaves as desired – they will last for about a month like this.

You can do the same thing with spring onions (scallions). Place 5 cm (2 inches) ends in a glass of water and watch a new flush of greens grow within a week. Keep changing the water every couple of days. I usually let them flourish twice until they reach about 20 cm (8 inches) and then discard them and rotate to a new batch, but you can always keep growing them in potted soil.

VEGETABLES

Save clean peelings for vegetable stock (you can even keep them in the freezer for another time) or deep-fry them to make crisps (chips) or chips (fries).

Always try to use the whole vegetable – broccoli stems and cauliflower leaves make great additions to recipes, providing lots of texture. They could go into curries, broths, rice porridge and noodle soups, or even the Easy Kimchi on page 207. If vegetable stalks (for example of Chinese mustard greens) are thick, slice them thinly before adding to the dish with the leaves. The thinner you slice something, the faster it will cook.

If poaching vegetables, wash them first and then reserve the delicious poaching water to make an additional seasoned soup with ginger, green leaves or whatever other vegetables you like. This poaching water is also great for making a quick rice porridge or for drinking as a hot or cold tea.

If all else fails, I use up older (safe) vegetables by giving them to the dog.

FRUIT

The sweetness in Vietnamese cooking comes mostly from sugar, but you can be very creative with flavour by using up soft ripe fruit (peaches, nectarines, kiwis, plums, berries, melon, mango, figs, grapes, etc.) in sauces instead of sugar. Simply remove any stones, pits or seeds, then mash or blend the fruit and add to your sauce to provide sweet and sour elements. Remember to always taste as you go.

Fruits are also delicious in savoury salads and adding harder fruits, such as apples and pears, to a broth is a great way of adding flavour without adding processed sugar.

To get the most out of a lemon, lime, orange or satsuma, zest it and use for sauces, salads and all types of recipes to add bitterness (so beware of its pungency) and zesty flavour.

FISH

When purchasing fish, ask the fishmonger to keep the heads. Freeze them to have on hand for whenever you need to make a delicious fish stock.

MEAT

The butcher usually has a lot of free bones, so ask for these when making a broth.

Reserve any fat, for example from the fatty cavity of a chicken, the rind of pork or trimmed from a steak, and render it down in a small saucepan over a low heat for about 10 minutes. Pour into a jar and keep for future cooking or use the chicken fat to make spring onion (scallion) oil (page 208). This fat is full of flavour and using it reduces the number of processed oils needed for cooking.

Use any leftover juices from roast chicken or pork to make gravy or reserve them for tossing through tomorrow's noodles.

1 SNACKS, SPEEDY LUNCHES & JOY

SNACKS, SPEEDY LUNCHES & JOY

At my supper clubs and dinner parties, I always make lots of snacks or starters. I see them as gifts that can be given to those I adore, so they can have something nice and tasty to share. These are good mood boosters. Depending on how many people I have coming or how many dishes I feel like cooking, I tend to prep way ahead of time so that when the guests arrive, I only have to finish things off or simply serve them.

These kinds of make-ahead snacks and dumplings are also fantastic for during the week, to eat while you wait for dinner to be ready too. I like having pre-made Prawn Tapioca Ravioli (page 30), Pork and Prawn Wontons (page 28) and Bao Buns (page 204) stashed in the freezer for this reason. Whenever I make them for an occasion, I always make sure to do some extra because I know I will really appreciate these little gifts to myself in the future. At the very least, I fill the freezer with shop-bought Chinese dumplings.

For a burst of adrenaline, I also like making Rice Paper Pizzas (page 35) on a gas hob (burner). I love the process of turning the paper with tongs, preventing it from catching fire and watching it crisp up. The crisp and crunch on these are so irresistible! Doing it with a friend usually causes a lot of laughter.

On days when it's just me at home in my kitchen, writing words and recipes or dealing with admin, I love to treat myself to a good sandwich, either a rice paper one with leftover vegetables or a toasted sandwich made in my panini press. I love cheese and vegetables and always try to use all the food groups in my meals. Sometimes, a great speedy meal would be a packet of ramen with a refrigerator raid of chives or coriander (cilantro) and leftover cold cuts if there are any, and perhaps some green leaves, too. I top it off with an egg, cracked in and poached in the soup while the noodles are cooking.

It is also great to have ready or even make a Lemongrass and Dill Chickpea Pâté (page 44) or Coriander Pesto (page 47) for a quick noodle or pasta lunch or just to slather on a fresh crusty baguette and eat alongside a glass of warm Soya Milk (page 195).

PORK AND PRAWN WONTONS

HOÀNH THÁNH

Makes 30 wontons

Prep time 30–40 minutes
Cook time 7–15 minutes

- 150 g (5½ oz) minced (ground) pork
- 200 g (7 oz) peeled raw king prawns (shrimp), finely chopped
- 100 g (3½ oz) tinned water chestnuts, finely chopped
- 2 spring onions (scallions), thinly sliced
- 2 tablespoons frozen edamame beans, defrosted
- 2 tablespoons oyster sauce
- pinch of sea salt
- 1 teaspoon caster (superfine) sugar
- ½ teaspoon freshly ground white pepper
- ½ tablespoon cornflour (cornstarch)
- 200 g (7 oz) square wonton wrappers (about 10 cm/4 inches)
- 2 teaspoons sesame oil, plus extra for drizzling
- 10 g (½ oz) garlic chives or coriander (cilantro) leaves, sliced into 3 cm (1¼ inch) pieces, to garnish (optional)

FOR THE DIPPING SAUCE

- 2 garlic cloves, finely chopped
- 2 bird's eye chillies, thinly sliced
- 2 teaspoons brown sugar
- 1 tablespoon black vinegar or cider vinegar
- 2 tablespoons light soy sauce
- 1 tablespoon crispy chilli oil

These can be enjoyed as a snack or starter. They also make a fantastic topping for noodle soups or even instant ramen. I always save uncooked ones for the freezer, then steam them from frozen for 10 minutes. I love to fold with a friend, and a cup of tea, so we can have a good catch-up.

First, make the dipping sauce by mixing together all the ingredients in a bowl.

Add the pork to another bowl with the chopped prawns, water chestnuts, spring onions, edamame beans, oyster sauce, salt, sugar and white pepper and mix well.

Lightly dust a plate with the cornflour and fill a cup with water. To form the dumplings, place a wrapper onto the palm of your hand and dollop 1 heaped teaspoon of filling into the middle. Moisten the edges of the wrapper with water. Fold the wonton wrapper over into a triangle while pushing the air out of the filling, then pinch the wrapper together to form a sack. Pinch and fan out the top to seal, then place on the prepared plate. Repeat until you have used up all the filling.

To cook the wontons, bring a large saucepan of water to the boil, then gently drop in a handful of wontons (don't crowd the pan) and let it come back to the boil. After 4–5 minutes the wontons will float to the surface. Cook for a further 2 minutes, then lift them out of the water with a spider or slotted spoon and place on a plate. Drizzle with sesame oil and repeat until you have cooked as many as you need. Keep any extras for freezing.

Garnish with the herbs, if using, then pour over the sauce or serve it on the side in dipping bowls.

Makes 20 dumplings

PRAWN TAPIOCA RAVIOLI WITH SWEET LIME AND CHILLI DRESSING

BÁNH BỘT LỌC TÔM

Prep time 20 minutes
Cook time 10 minutes

FOR THE PRAWN FILLING

- 150 g (5½ oz) peeled raw king prawns (shrimp), patted dry
- ¼ teaspoon sea salt
- ¼ teaspoon caster (superfine) sugar
- ¼ teaspoon mushroom seasoning powder

FOR THE SPRING ONION OIL

- 3 tablespoons olive oil
- 4 spring onions (scallions), thinly sliced

FOR THE SWEET LIME AND CHILLI DRESSING

- juice of ½ lime
- 2 tablespoons caster (superfine) sugar
- 2 tablespoons premium fish sauce
- 2 bird's eye chillies, thinly sliced on the diagonal

FOR THE DOUGH

- 200 g (7 oz/1¾ cup) tapioca flour, plus extra for dusting
- 150 ml (5 fl oz/scant ⅔ cup) boiling water

NOTE

Once the ravioli has been filled, these can be stored in the refrigerator for up to 2 days, ready to be cooked just before serving.

These are a street food speciality in my mum's hometown, Phan Thiết. They are slippery and chewy with the perfect crunch of fresh prawns (shrimp). I think my dad married my mum because he loved these as much as he did her. They are great to prep ahead for dinner parties, as you can refrigerate them and then just cook them when ready to serve. Different brands of tapioca flour will vary in texture and how they absorb hot water, so you might need to add tiny bit more if it looks dry.

Put the prawns into a bowl and season with the salt, sugar and mushroom seasoning. Set aside in the refrigerator.

Next, make the spring onion oil. Combine the olive oil and spring onions in a small saucepan over a medium heat. Cook for 1 minute, then remove from the heat and set aside.

Make the dressing by mixing together all the ingredients in a bowl. Stir well until the sugar dissolves.

To make the dough, put the tapioca flour into a bowl. Slowly pour the boiling water around the bowl. Quickly mix together with a wooden spoon. Once it forms a rough dough, tip it out onto a lightly dusted work surface or wooden cutting board and knead for 5 minutes until it forms a smooth ball, similar to fondant icing. If it is dry, add a further 2 teaspoons of boiling hot water.

Roll the dough into a sausage and cut it in half, then divide each half into 10 pieces. Roll out one of the pieces into a disc about 3 mm (1/10 inch) thick and 8 cm (3 inches) in diameter.

Place a prawn in the middle of the disc and fold the dough over to create a half-moon, then pinch the edges together. Feel free to use the crinkly side of a cookie cutter to make pretty edges. Set aside, then repeat with the remaining dough and filling.

To cook the ravioli, bring a large saucepan of water to the boil, then gently drop in some of the ravioli one by one and let it come back to the boil. Prevent them from sticking together by separating them with a pair of chopsticks. After about 3 minutes the ravioli will float to the surface. Cook for a further 1 minute, then lift them out of the water with a spider or slotted spoon and place on a plate.

Quickly smother them with the spring onion oil to prevent them from sticking and then pour over the sweet lime and chilli dressing.

Makes 1

GRILLED CHEESE BAGUETTE WITH SARDINES AND KIMCHI

BÁNH MÌ NƯỚNG PHÔ MAI CÁ MÒI VÀ KIM CHI

Prep time 5 minutes
Cook time 5 minutes

- 1 x 18 cm (7 inch) baguette or panini
- ½ x 120 g (4¼ oz) tin of sardines (in olive oil, tomato sauce or whatever you like)
- 20 g (¾ oz) Cheddar, sliced (or any hard cheese)
- 1 heaped tablespoon kimchi (shop-bought or homemade, page 207)
- watercress and tomato salad, to serve

Tinned sardines are a must-have in my pantry because you can always make a meal out of them. Sometimes I even carry them around in my handbag so I can stuff them into a fresh baguette for lunch! They are also great for a simple meal with steamed rice, a bit of kimchi and some vegetables.

For a quick, very filling and satisfying lunch, I like to make this sandwich. Add a side salad and an Artichoke Tea (page 192) for a perfect, complete meal.

Preheat a panini press or toasted sandwich grill.

Slice open the baguette and scrape out some of the bread interior. Mash and spread the sardines onto the bread, then layer the Cheddar on top. Evenly spread the kimchi over the other side of the baguette. Sandwich together.

Place the sandwich in the panini press and cook for about 5 minutes, or until the cheese is melted and bubbling. (If you don't have a panini press, place the sandwich on a hot griddle pan and press with a steak or chef's press or weigh down with something heavy. Alternatively, bake the sandwich in a 200°C fan/425°F oven for 5 minutes.)

Serve immediately with the watercress and tomato salad.

Makes 4 pizzas

RICE PAPER PIZZAS WITH EGGS, SPINACH AND SARDINES

BÁNH TRÁNG NƯỚNG TRỨNG RAU VÀ CÁ MÒI

Prep time 15 minutes
Cook time 40 minutes

½ tablespoon olive oil
200 g (7 oz) spinach leaves
8 x 20–22 cm (8–8½ inches) sheets of rice paper
4 small eggs
1 x 120 g (4¼ oz) tin of sardines in tomato sauce or 1 x 50 g (1¾ oz) tin of anchovies, coarsely mashed
handful of rocket (arugula)

FOR THE GARLIC BUTTER SAUCE

20 g (¾ oz) salted butter
4 garlic cloves, sliced
4 teaspoons capers
1 teaspoon chilli (hot pepper) flakes
1 tablespoon premium fish sauce
1 teaspoon sesame oil

FOR THE SPRING ONION OIL

2 tablespoons olive oil
2 spring onions (scallions), sliced
pinch of sea salt

I like to cut these into triangles to make canapés for sharing among a crowd. They should remain crisp for a while. Otherwise, they can be served whole or folded up and enjoyed like a crêpe or calzone. To make this easier, arrange your workspace like a pizza station with the ingredients handy in bowls. They are a fun job to share with kids or party guests, as they can compile the pizza and you can cook them.

First, pour the ½ tablespoon of the olive oil into a frying pan over a medium heat and wilt the spinach. Leave for 5 minutes to cool, then squeeze out the water with your hands or in a clean dish towel and set aside.

Make the garlic butter sauce. Melt the butter in a small frying pan over a medium heat, then fry the garlic for about 1 minute until sizzling. Add the capers and chilli flakes and stir to combine, then add the fish sauce and sesame oil. Cook for a further minute, then remove from the heat and set aside.

Next, make a spring onion oil for brushing the rice paper. Pour the 2 tablespoons of olive oil into a small saucepan over a medium heat. Add the spring onions and salt and cook for a couple minutes until the green parts of the onions start to wilt, then remove from the heat and set aside.

Use a pastry brush to paint one side of the rice paper sheets with the spring onion oil, then place another sheet on top. Place each rice paper 'sandwich' between two chopping boards and press down to help them stick together.

If you have a gas hob (burner), place a wire rack over a low flame and place one of the rice paper sandwiches on top. Scatter some of the spinach over the top, then crack an egg in the middle. Dot around some of the sardines or anchovies. Cook for 5–8 minutes, continuously moving the paper around in circles with tongs to prevent it from burning. The egg should be cooked with a runny yolk and the edges of the pizza should be crispy and slightly puffy.

If you don't have a gas hob, cook the pizza in a dry frying pan over a medium-high heat for 5–8 minutes. Alternatively, you can cook it under a medium-high grill in an ovenproof frying pan for 4–6 minutes.

When the pizza is cooked, scatter the top with rocket and drizzle over the garlic butter sauce. Serve immediately.

Makes 1

Prep time 5 minutes
Cook time 5–7 minutes

- 1 x 20–22 cm (8–8½ inch) sheet of rice paper
- 3 thin slices of aubergine (eggplant)
- 1 small or medium egg, beaten
- 1 teaspoon light soy sauce
- 1 spring onion (scallion), sliced lengthways
- sprig of coriander (cilantro)
- 1 teaspoon crispy chilli oil
- additional fillings of your choice, such as vegetables or leftovers

RICE PAPER SANDWICH

BÁNH GỐI

This is a super-fast and delicious snack that uses leftovers and storecupboard ingredients. Thinly slice any vegetables you have and add those, add spoonfuls of veggie or meat leftovers or dot with savoury spreads. Be as creative as you would when making a bread sandwich. Mix and match to your heart's content!

Put the sheet of rice paper into a dry frying pan over a medium heat. Add the aubergine slices (and any other fillings you might be using), pour the egg into the middle, splash the soy sauce over the top and sprinkle over the spring onions. Cook for about 5–7 minutes until the egg is cooked, then dot over the coriander and crispy chilli oil.

Fold the pancake over (and fold again into quarters if you like) and serve immediately.

維他
250 mL 8.45 fl oz

LEMONGRASS AND VEGETABLE FRITTER BÁNH MÌ

BÁNH MÌ RAU CỦ CHIÊN ƯỚP SẢ

Makes 6 sandwiches

Prep time 25 minutes
Cook time 20 minutes

FOR THE SAUCE

- 1–2 teaspoons English or Dijon mustard, according to taste
- 1 tablespoon ginger preserve, marmalade or apricot jam
- 1½ tablespoons Yondu vegetable umami sauce or premium fish sauce
- 1 tablespoon lime juice
- 1 bird's eye chilli, finely chopped
- 1 onion, very finely diced

FOR THE VEGETABLE MIX

- 2 small round shallots, sliced
- 4 garlic cloves, grated
- 20 g (¾ oz) lemongrass, finely chopped
- 80 g (2¾ oz) carrot, julienned
- 130 g (4½ oz) courgette (zucchini), julienned
- 50 g (1¾ oz) okra, thinly sliced
- 1 spring onion, sliced lengthways
- 2 tablespoons nutritional yeast
- 1 tablespoon premium fish sauce or 1 teaspoon fermented tofu, mashed

FOR THE BATTER

- 70 g (2½ oz/generous ⅓ cup) rice flour
- ½ teaspoon baking powder
- 70 g (2½ oz/generous ¼ cup) coconut or plain yoghurt
- 4 tablespoons water
- ¼ teaspoon sea salt

TO SERVE

- 6 Vietnamese baguettes or crusty bread rolls
- neutral oil, for deep-frying
- 6 Laughing Cow cheese triangles (or mayonnaise or butter) (optional)
- fillings of choice
- 6 tablespoons kimchi (shop-bought or homemade, page 207) or sliced gherkins
- mint and corianser sprigs

This is a great weekend lunch (especially when served with homemade chips/French fries, page 164). It is delightful way to eat more plants as it can be filled with any herbs and vegetables, such as lettuce, gherkins, mint, tomato, cucumber and coriander. Crusty white rolls serve as a great alternative to Vietnamese baguettes. Alternatively, make small fritter balls to have as a starter or snack or use them to fill Bao Buns (page 204).

If you don't want to make six sandwiches, you can store the vegetable batter mixture in the refrigerator for up to 2 days. Any leftover cooked fritters can be reheated in a very hot oven for 5 minutes.

First, mix all the sauce ingredients together in a bowl, then set aside.

Put all of the ingredients for the vegetable mix into a bowl and toss together, then set aside.

Whisk together all the ingredients for the batter in a large bowl until thick and smooth.

Pour 4 cm (1½ inches) oil into a wok or large frying pan and bring up to 180°C (350°F).

Combine the vegetable mix with the batter and divide into six portions. Scoop a portion onto a large kitchen spoon or slotted spoon and squash it to form a round burger shape with the back of a tablespoon. Slide it into the oil and fry for 6 minutes, two at a time, flipping every couple of minutes, until golden on both sides. Remove and drain on paper towels. Repeat with the remaining vegetable and batter mixture.

Split and grill or toast the baguettes or rolls. Spread with the cheese, then layers of fillings, such as a lettuce leaf, tomato and cucumber slices, then a vegetable fritter. Spread some of the sauce over it, then cover with kimchi or gherkin slices and add mint and coriander on top. Serve immediately for ultimate freshness. If serving later, cool the fritters to room temperature.

Makes 4–5 pancakes

RICE FLOUR AND COCONUT VEGETABLE PANCAKES

BÁNH XÈO HÀN QUỐC CHAY

Prep time 20 minutes
Cook time 30 minutes

FOR THE DIPPING SAUCE

- 1 tablespoon Yondu vegetable umami sauce, premium fish sauce or light soy sauce
- 2 teaspoons cider vinegar
- 2 teaspoons maple syrup
- 1 teaspoon toasted sesame seeds (optional)
- 1 teaspoon gochujang (optional)

FOR THE BATTER

- 150 g (5½ oz/generous ¾ cup) rice flour
- 4 tablespoons cornflour (cornstarch)
- 2 teaspoons sea salt
- ¼ teaspoon ground turmeric
- 150 ml (5 fl oz/scant ⅔ cup) coconut milk
- 150 ml (5 fl oz/scant ⅔ cup) cold sparkling water

FOR THE TOPPINGS

- 2 small round shallots, sliced
- 100 g (3½ oz) red cabbage, thinly sliced or shredded
- 100 g (3½ oz) carrot, julienned
- 6 asparagus, sliced into quarters lengthways
- 100 g (3½ oz) cauliflower, thinly sliced
- 2 tablespoons olive oil
- 6–8 spring onions (scallions), halved to fit the pan, sliced lengthways
- kimchi (shop-bought or homemade, page 207), to serve (optional)
- microgreens of your choice, to serve (optional)

Similar to Korean *jeon* pancakes or Japanese *okonomiyaki*, but even crispier, these gorgeous pancakes are filled with the kinds of vegetables I always have in the refrigerator. You can use any veg you like but be mindful that vegetables with a higher water content, like mushrooms or courgettes (zucchini), can make your pancake less crispy. This is brilliant as a starter or for lunch and it's a fantastic way to get you eating all sorts of combinations of vegetables. I enjoy this with a side of kimchi and, while it's great without any toppings, it is excellent with a sprinkling of microgreens such as pea shoots, coriander (cilantro), mint, radicchio or sprouts.

First, make the dipping sauce by mixing together all the ingredients in a bowl.

Put all the batter ingredients into a large bowl, whisk to combine, then add the shallots, cabbage, carrot, asparagus and cauliflower. Mix well to coat the vegetables in the batter.

Heat the oil in a roughly 20 cm (8 inch) frying pan over a medium-high heat. Spread a generous layer of spring onions onto the pan, then use a large spoon to scoop about a quarter of the batter mixture into the pan. Spread it out and flatten it to fill the pan.

Fry for 3–5 minutes until golden on the underside, then flip and fry on the other side for a further 3 minutes. Remove from the pan and repeat with the remaining mixture.

To serve, lay the pancakes on a plate and use scissors to cut them into bite-sized squares. Serve immediately with the dipping sauce and kimchi and microgreens, if using.

Serves 4

BATTERED SPRING ONIONS

BÁNH HÀNH CHIÊN

Prep time 12 minutes
Cook time 20 minutes

- 150 g (5½ oz/scant 1¼ cups) plain (all-purpose) flour
- 50 g (1¾ oz/scant ½ cup) cornflour (cornstarch)
- 1 teaspoon baking powder
- 1 teaspoon garlic powder
- 1 teaspoon nigella seeds or sesame seeds (optional)
- 1 teaspoon sea salt, plus extra to serve
- neutral oil, for frying
- 200 ml (7 fl oz/scant 1 cup) very cold sparkling water or beer
- 20 spring onions (scallions), trimmed and sliced into 15 cm (6 inch) lengths
- freshly ground black pepper
- 1 teaspoon shichimi tōgarashi (Japanese red pepper seasoning; optional)

FOR THE CORIANDER DIPPING SAUCE

- 50 g (1¾ oz) coriander (cilantro), leaves and stalks
- 20 g (¾ oz) fresh ginger root, peeled and grated
- 1 garlic clove
- 100 g (3½ oz/generous ⅓ cup) coconut or plain yoghurt
- zest and juice of ½ lime or lemon
- 1 teaspoon chilli (hot pepper) flakes or powder (optional)
- a pinch of sea salt

Spring onions (scallions) are cheap and delicious – especially if they are homegrown. I regrow my spring onion ends in a glass of water (page 22), making them even more thrifty. These battered spring onions make a great posh onion ring-style starter or snack and they are brilliant as a filling for *bánh mì*, too (page 39). The batter can also be used to deep-fry other vegetables such as courgettes (zucchini), carrots, pumpkin, asparagus and so on.

First, make the dipping sauce. Combine all the ingredients in a food processor and blend until smooth. Scrape out and set aside. If you don't have a food processor, finely chop or bash the coriander, ginger and garlic in a mortar and pestle then combine with the rest of the ingredients.

Put the flour and cornflour into a large bowl and add the baking powder, garlic powder, nigella or sesame seeds, if using, and salt.

Pour 4 cm (1½ inches) oil into a wok and bring up to 180°C (350°F).

When the oil is at the right temperature, add the cold sparkling water or beer to the batter. Whisk to combine, then add the spring onions and stir to coat in the batter.

Fry a few spring onions at a time (don't overcrowd the pan) for 2–3 minutes until golden and crisp, flipping if necessary. Remove with a spider or slotted spoon and place on a wire rack to drain. Immediately season with salt and pepper, then repeat with the rest of the spring onions.

Before serving, sprinkle the spring onions with the shichimi tōgarashi, if using. Serve with the coriander dipping sauce.

Makes 2 x
350 g (12 oz) jars

LEMONGRASS AND DILL CHICKPEA PÂTÉ

PÂTÉ CHAY

Prep time 15 minutes

- 250 g (9 oz) drained chickpeas, butter (lima) beans or haricot (navy) beans
- 1 garlic cloves, finely chopped
- 1 shallot, diced
- 1 tablespoon nutritional yeast or ½ teaspoon mushroom seasoning powder
- ¼ teaspoon ground white pepper
- ¼ teaspoon freshly ground black pepper
- 2 tablespoons extra virgin olive oil, plus extra for storing
- 10 g (½ oz) lemongrass, finely chopped
- 1 teaspoon premium fish sauce or Yondu vegetable umami sauce
- 5 g (¼ oz) dill or coriander (cilantro) leaves, sliced
- 1 bird's eye chilli, thinly sliced (optional)
- zest and juice of ¾ lime

This dip mimics the taste of the famous Hà Nôi fishcakes (page 136). It is so good as a spread on crusty bread to enjoy with a soup or to have on toast for breakfast and it's also fantastic spread on Rice Paper Pizzas (page 35) or sandwiches.

Combine all the ingredients, except the lime juice, in a food processor and blend until smooth. Add half the lime juice and blend again, then taste and see if it needs more.

Scrape into clean jars, then cover with a layer of oil and screw on the lids.

Serve with lots of extra lime juice as a dip with a plate of crudités or as a spread for toast or a sandwich filling.

Serves 4

CORIANDER PESTO

SỐT NGÒ

Prep time 10 minutes

- 30 g (1 oz/⅓ cup) desiccated (dried shredded) coconut, pine nuts, cashews, almonds, pistachio or peanuts
- 60 g (2 oz) coriander (cilantro), with stalks, chopped
- 4 tablespoons extra virgin olive oil, plus 2 tablespoons to top up
- 4 tablespoons nutritional yeast
- zest and juice of ½ lemon or lime
- 1 teaspoon sea salt
- 2 garlic cloves, sliced

This is a luxurious dip with crudités, which is great slathered on a baguette, brilliant tossed with blanched vegetables and tofu or for dressing a salad and it is, of course, perfect with any pasta or noodles.

Put all the ingredients, except for the 2 tablespoons of extra virgin olive oil, into bowl or small food processor and blend to a pale green, grainy pesto-like consistency.

Transfer to a clean jar and top with the 2 tablespoons of extra virgin olive oil to conserve the pesto. Store in the refrigerator for up to 7 days.

2 SALAD & VEGETABLES

SALAD & VEGETABLES

There are some moments when you suddenly feel an enormous gratitude for being alive. It might be the warm breeze you feel when cycling on a summer evening or the sun setting on your face as you catch whiffs of jasmine and lavender in the air. Or maybe it's dipping into the sea for the first time in a year and feeling the cool, cleansing water wash over you. Or, perhaps it comes on Friday evenings as you swig down the first sip of an ice-cold beer. To me, salads and vegetables add this feeling to meals.

My favourite place to shop is the greengrocer – it's where I explore dinner's possibilities. I might pick up a purple sweet potato for steaming and eating for fun or to add to a rice pudding. I will pick up Delica pumpkin for curries, purple-skinned kohlrabi for a stir-fried side dish (page 59), beautiful bouquets of radicchio and colourful autumn lettuces for summer rolls (page 146) and wraps.

I tend to buy produce only for the next 3 days, going to all my local shops. I love hand-picking what I want, behaving exactly like my mother, inhaling the scent of melons and making sure I gather nothing old or bad. Every detail is valuable to the perfect meal.

CHICKEN SALAD WITH MUSHROOM RICE

GỎI GÀ BẮP CẢI VÀ CƠM NẤM

Serves 4–5

Prep time 20 minutes
Cook time 1 hour

1.6 litres (54 fl oz/6¾ cups) water
1.6 kg (3 lb 8½ oz) chicken
1 tablespoon sea salt
15 g (½ oz) rock sugar
300 g (10½ oz) jasmine or basmati rice, washed three times
1 chicken stock cube
100 g (3½ oz) chestnut (cremini) mushrooms, chopped or sliced
ferments or pickles, to serve

FOR THE DRESSING

2 bird's eye chillies, finely chopped
3 tablespoons clear honey
3 tablespoons premium fish sauce
3 tablespoons extra virgin olive oil
30 g (1 oz) fresh ginger root, peeled and grated
zest of 1 lemon or lime, plus 3 tablespoons juice

FOR THE SALAD

150 g (5½ oz) sugar snap peas, de-stringed and thinly sliced lengthways
125 g (4½ oz) red cabbage, thinly sliced
80 g (2¾ oz) coriander (cilantro) or Vietnamese coriander (cilantro), roughly sliced

There are so many wonderful ways to enjoy chicken and rice. This dish plays with the silky, meaty texture of the chicken against the crunchy textures of the salad. A cold salad served on hot, warming mushroom rice is the perfect way to comfort yourself on those colder autumn evenings, reminding you of the prospect of warmer spring afternoons.

Pour the water into a large saucepan and bring to the boil, then add the chicken, salt and sugar. Cover and simmer for 30 minutes, then remove from the heat and let it cook in the residual heat for a further 30 minutes. Remove the chicken (reserving the broth) and transfer to a bowl of cold water for at least 15 minutes.

Meanwhile, put the rice into a rice cooker with 500 ml (17 fl oz/ generous 2 cups) of the chicken broth, the chicken stock cube and mushrooms. Cook on the cook setting, then fluff up the rice with a rice paddle or fork and set aside for at least 10 minutes on the 'keep warm' setting.

If you don't have a rice cooker, simmer the ingredients in a saucepan over a medium-low heat for 8 minutes with a lid on. Once the water has mostly been absorbed by the rice, reduce the heat to low and cook for a further 18 minutes. Remove from the heat, fluff up the rice and keep covered for a further 10 minutes.

Make the dressing by mixing together all the ingredients in a small bowl.

Put the sugar snap peas, red cabbage and coriander into another bowl. Tear the chicken along the grain and add to the salad. Add the dressing and toss together.

Serve the salad with the mushroom rice and a side of ferments or pickles.

NOTE

For a lovely warming and soothing side, season the remaining broth with fish sauce and add some sliced spring onions (scallions) or 200 g (7 oz) watercress or spinach.

Serves 4

LEAFY ORANGE AND GINGER SALAD WITH MARINATED ARTICHOKES

GỎI CAM GỪNG VÀ HOA ATISÔ

Prep time 10 minutes

½ head of radicchio
60 g (2 oz) watercress
1 golden beetroot (beet), peeled and julienned
8 marinated artichokes, quartered
1 carrot, peeled into ribbons
2 satsumas or 1 orange, segmented and halved
1 kiwi, peeled, quartered and sliced
handful of blackberries (optional)
20 g (¾ oz) coriander (cilantro) or mint leaves, roughly torn

FOR THE DRESSING

20 g (¾ oz) fresh ginger root, peeled and grated
1 carrot, very finely grated (using the zesting side of the grater)
zest and juice of 1 orange
zest and juice of ½ lime
1 tablespoon clear honey
2 tablespoons light soy sauce or premium fish sauce
1 tbsp extra virgin olive oil

This is really good as a side salad, tossed with noodles or with a buttered crusty baguette or ciabatta. Fresh artichokes are usually enjoyed as tea in Vietnam, but I often pick up a jar of meaty marinated artichokes from the deli – they are a great option for meat-free days. You can use this lovely dressing with a variety of leaves, herbs and fruit and vegetables.

Mix together all the dressing ingredients in a bowl.

Combine the rest of the ingredients, except the coriander or mint, in a large bowl, then add the dressing and toss together. Garnish with the herbs before serving.

Makes 8

SALMON AND AVOCADO SUMMER ROLLS

GỎI CUỐN CÁ HỒI VỚI BƠ

Prep time 20 minutes
Cook time 25 minutes

- 1 yellow or red beetroot (beets), peeled and sliced into 5 mm (¼ inch) thick rings
- 1 teaspoon olive oil
- 200 g (7 oz) skinless salmon fillets
- 3 tablespoons teriyaki sauce
- 8 x 22 cm (8½ inch) sheets of rice paper
- 2 ripe avocados, sliced
- 20 cm (8 inch) cucumber, cut into batons
- 8 sprigs of dill, finely chopped
- 8 sprigs of coriander (cilantro)
- 16 mint leaves
- 160 g (5½ oz) 0.8 mm rice vermicelli, soaked in boiling water for 10 minutes, then drained, rinsed in hot water and cooled to room temperature in a colander with a cover

FOR THE DIPPING SAUCE

- ½ tablespoon extra virgin olive oil
- 2 garlic cloves, finely chopped
- 1 bird's eye chilli, finely chopped
- 2 tablespoons smooth or crunchy peanut, cashew or almond butter
- 1½ tablespoons premium fish sauce
- 1 tablespoon maple syrup or clear honey
- 1 tablespoon cider vinegar
- 2 tablespoons water
- 2 tablespoons roasted and salted peanuts, roughly chopped

Everybody's favourite gift to the mouth, *gỏi cuốn* translates as 'rolled salad'. I fill mine with tons of herbs and vegetables, but you can pick and choose from what you have. This fantastic combination is made even more pleasurable by the silky and moreish nutty dipping sauce.

Preheat the oven to 200°C fan (425°F).

Spread the slices of beetroot out on a baking tray (pan), brush over the olive oil and bake for 8 minutes.

Place the salmon onto a baking sheet lined with parchment paper and spread over the teriyaki sauce. Add to the oven and bake the salmon and beetroot for a further 12–15 minutes. Remove and set aside to cool to room temperature, then flake the salmon with a fork.

Meanwhile, make the dipping sauce. Heat the oil in a small saucepan over a medium-low heat and add the garlic and chilli. Once the garlic has turned slightly golden and released its fragrance (about a minute), add the nut butter. Mix the butter in to melt it and stir until it is lump-free. Add the fish sauce, maple syrup or honey, cider vinegar and water. Mix well to combine, then remove from the heat. Serve in individual dipping bowls, sprinkled with the peanuts.

To make the rolls, dip a sheet of rice paper for a second into water to moisten it, then transfer to a board or large plate. Just below the middle of the paper, line up a couple of slices of avocado, beetroot, cucumber and flaked salmon. Top with some dill, coriander and mint and a thin layer of noodles.

Fold the left and the right sides in by approximately 3–4 cm (1¼–1½ inches), then fold the bottom flap over the filling and roll up tightly and firmly, tucking in all the ingredients with your fingers as you go.

Repeat with the remaining ingredients, then serve with the dipping sauce.

Serves 4

STIR-FRIED KOHLRABI WITH CHOPPED PRAWNS AND CHIVES

SU SU XÀO TÔM

Prep time 10 minutes
Cook time 10 minutes

- 1½ tablespoons rapeseed (canola) oil or olive oil
- 4 garlic cloves, finely chopped
- 2 kohlrabi, peeled and thinly sliced into half-moons
- 15 g (½ oz) salted butter
- 1 tablespoon oyster sauce
- 200 g (7 oz) cooked prawns (shrimp), chopped into 1 cm (½ inch) pieces
- 20 g (¾ oz) chives, sliced into 5 cm (2 inch) lengths
- freshly ground black pepper
- zest and juice of ¼ lemon or lime
- chilli (hot pepper) flakes, sliced bird's eye chillies or crispy chilli oil (optional)

All different types of harder, crunchy vegetables can be used in this recipe, such as chayote, courgette (zucchini) or any great autumn crops such as pears, apples, fennel, cauliflower and so on. You can use a mix of them, too. Slice the vegetables thinly so that they cook faster but still have some bite to them. My cousin Thảo in Vietnam loves to fry cucumbers in this way. I like to serve this with steamed rice for a quick midweek dinner. It's particularly good with the Pan-fried Fish with Green Mango on page 59.

Heat the oil in a wok or large frying pan over a high heat and fry the garlic for 1 minute until fragrant and starting to turn golden. Immediately add the kohlrabi and wait for 30 seconds, then stir-fry vigorously. Add the butter and oyster sauce then continue to stir-fry for 3 minutes. Add the chopped prawns and chives, season with black pepper and toss the pan for a minute.

Add the lemon or lime zest and juice, then serve with chilli flakes, bird's eye chillies or crispy chilli oil, if desired.

Serves 4

KING PRAWN AND MANGO RICE PAPER SALAD

BÁNH TRẮNG TRỘN TÔM XOÀI

Prep time 15 minutes
Cook time 15 minutes

- 400 ml (14 fl oz/generous 1½ cups) coconut water or water
- 8 raw shell-on king prawns (shrimp), trimmed
- 1 unripe mango, peeled and cut into thin moons
- 1 beetroot (beet), julienned (any kind, but just be mindful of the red bleed) (optional)
- 100 g (3½ oz) sugar snap peas, sliced lengthways
- 8 quail's eggs, cooked, peeled and halved
- 4 x 22 cm (8½ inch) sheets of rice paper, snipped into 3 cm (1¼ inch) strips
- 1 tablespoon dried shrimp, coarsely ground in mortar and pestle (optional)
- 2 tablespoons Crispy Shallots (page 208, or use shop-bought)
- 40 g (1½ oz) Vietnamese coriander (cilantro) or Thai basil
- 1 tablespoon toasted peanuts or cashews, roughly chopped

FOR THE DRESSING

- 40 g (1½ oz) tamarind paste
- 2 tablespoons soft brown sugar
- 100 ml (3½ fl oz/scant ½ cup) boiling water
- 2 tablespoons premium fish sauce
- 1 small round shallot, finely diced
- 1 bird's eye chilli, sliced diagonally
- 2 tablespoons roasted peanuts or cashews, roughly chopped

Use any variety of seafood or meat for this dish, such as langoustines or leftover cold cuts, or make it veggie-friendly by using marinated artichokes, dried or fresh figs and crispy fried tofu. It is great as a starter, or you can make it a complete meal with steamed rice or sticky rice. It is also great on rice vermicelli noodles.

First, make the dressing. Put the tamarind paste and sugar into a bowl and pour over the boiling water. Set aside for 5 minutes, then break up any chunks of paste with a spoon and mix thoroughly. Pass the mixture through a sieve (fine mesh strainer), then add the fish sauce, shallot and chilli.

Pour the coconut water into a saucepan and bring to the boil, then add the prawns and swirl the water around. Cover and cook for 2–3 minutes until the prawns are pink and opaque. Drain and set aside to cool to room temperature.

Combine the green mango, beetroot, sugar snap peas, quail's eggs, prawns and strips of rice paper in a large bowl.

Mix the nuts into the dressing, then drizzle some over the salad and toss until the rice papers have softened.

Finish with the dried shrimp (if using), crispy shallots, herbs and extra nuts. Use the remaining dressing for dipping the king prawns once peeled.

Serves 4

WILD CORNISH SARDINE SALAD

Prep time 15 minutes
Cook time 5–10 minutes

100 g (3½ oz) watercress
4–6 pickled beetroot (beets), sliced into thin rounds
8–12 cherry tomatoes, halved or quartered
10 g (½ oz) mint leaves
1 tablespoon extra virgin olive oil
300 g (10½ oz) sardines, butterflied and patted dry with paper towels
sea salt and freshly ground black pepper
4 slices of sourdough bread
10 g (½ oz) salted butter
juice of ½ lemon or lime
lemon wedges, to serve

FOR THE DRESSING

1 garlic clove, peeled
1 bird's eye chilli
200 g (7 oz) tinned pineapple with its juice
zest of 1 lemon or lime, plus 1 tablespoon of juice
1 tablespoon premium fish sauce
1 tablespoon extra virgin olive oil

This salad touches on every part of the palate. Peppery and crunchy watercress pairs so well with the succulent sardines and juicy, sweet tomatoes. The citrus adds zing and the chewy, buttery sourdough provides texture. Feel free to use more or a different variety of leaves or add any pickles or ferments you fancy. Kimchi or sauerkraut works well.

First, make the dressing. Put all the ingredients into a food processor and blend until smooth. Alternatively, bash the garlic, chilli and pineapple together in a mortar and pestle, then mix with the pineapple juice, lemon or lime zest and juice, fish sauce and oil.

Divide the watercress, beetroot, tomatoes and mint leaves between plates and drizzle over half the dressing.

Heat the oil a non-stick frying pan over a medium heat and cook the sardines, skin side down, for 2 minutes. Season with salt and pepper, then flip and cook the other side for 2 minutes. Remove from the heat and leave to rest in the pan for 5 minutes.

Meanwhile, toast the bread, then butter it and cut it into bite-sized squares. Scatter the pieces onto the salad plates, then place the sardines on top. Squeeze over the lemon or lime juice and serve immediately.

Serves 4

SWEET AND SOUR CRISPY TOFU WITH GREEN BEANS

TÀU HỦ CHUA NGỌT

Prep time 10 minutes
Cook time 25 minutes

- 5 tablespoons cornflour (cornstarch)
- ¼ teaspoon sea salt
- ¼ teaspoon garlic powder
- 600 g (1 lb 5 oz) medium-firm tofu, cut into 3 cm (1¼ inch) squares and patted dry with paper towels
- 3 tablespoons vegetable oil
- 2 tablespoons rapeseed (canola) oil
- 2 garlic cloves, finely chopped
- 15 g (½ oz) ginger, finely chopped
- 1 small white onion, sliced into 1 cm (½ inch) wide strips
- ½ red (bell) pepper, sliced into 1 cm (½ inch) wide strips
- 150–200 g (5½–7 oz) green beans, trimmed
- 2 spring onions (scallions), sliced into 5 cm (2 inch) lengths

FOR THE SAUCE

- ½ tablespoon cornflour (cornstarch) mixed with 2 tablespoons water
- 2 tablespoons ketchup
- 2 tablespoons chilli sauce (optional)
- 2 tablespoons rice vinegar
- 2 tablespoons premium fish sauce
- 1 teaspoon brown sugar (optional)
- 2 tablespoons crispy chilli oil

OPTIONAL GARNISHES

- coriander (cilantro) or Thai basil leaves
- chopped cashews or peanuts
- sliced red or bird's eye chillies

I love the way tofu soaks up and carries flavour. Here the tofu mimicks chicken nuggets in a kind of naughty fakeaway-style yet makes you relish the benefits of plant-based ingredients. This is also great with Tenderstem broccoli (broccolini) or a mixture of any crunchy vegetables and herbs.

First, make the sauce by mixing together all the ingredients in a bowl, then set aside.

Combine the cornflour, salt and garlic powder in a bowl, then add the tofu and gently toss to coat.

Heat the vegetable oil in a medium frying pan over a medium heat and fry the tofu chunks for about 4 minutes on each side until the bottoms turn golden. Drain on paper towels, then repeat with the remaining tofu.

Discard the vegetable oil and add the rapeseed oil to the same pan. Fry the garlic and ginger over a medium-high heat for 2 minutes until fragrant and starting to colour, then add the onion, red pepper, green beans and spring onions. Cook, stirring occasionally, for 3–4 minutes until charred in places.

Stir the sauce, then pour into the pan and stir-fry for 3–4 minutes until the sauce thickens. Add the fried tofu and stir for about 30 seconds to coat everything with the sauce. Serve immediately with your desired garnishes.

PLUMMY AUBERGINES

CÀ TÍM XỐT MẬN

Serves 4

Prep time 10 minutes
Cook time 20 minutes

- 2 aubergines (eggplants)
- 2 tablespoons olive oil
- 2 teaspoons ghee
- 4 garlic cloves, crushed or finely chopped
- 1–2 bird's eye chillies, finely chopped
- 20 g (¾ oz) spring onions (scallions), thinly sliced lengthways
- 3–4 tablespoons plum sauce (shop-bought or homemade, see introduction)
- 2 tablespoons premium fish sauce or light soy sauce
- 1 tablespoon thinly sliced coriander (cilantro) stalks
- 1 teaspoon toasted sesame seeds
- zest and juice of ½ lime

If you have a good stash of seasonal plums, blitz them in a food processor and then pass them through a sieve (fine mesh strainer), adding sugar if needed. The resulting purée is a great addition to sauces and for giving dishes a fruity, sweet flavour profile. This is great served as a side dish or enjoyed on steamed rice or with Vermicelli Noodle Salad Bowls (page 210).

Slice the aubergines lengthways into four thick slices. Using a sharp knife, score 3 mm (⅛ inch) deep lines into the flesh on each side in a criss-cross pattern. Brush the olive oil all over the sides of the aubergines.

Heat a large, dry frying pan over a high heat and sear the aubergine pieces for 5 minutes on each side. Remove from the pan and transfer to a serving plate.

Heat the ghee in a small saucepan over a medium heat and fry the garlic and chillies for 1 minute until it starts to colour, then add the spring onions, plum sauce and fish or soy sauce. Simmer for 2–3 minutes until well combined, then pour over the aubergines. To serve, scatter over the coriander stalks and toasted sesame seeds and then squeeze over the lime juice and sprinkle over the zest.

NOTE

If you want to prep this ahead of time, sear the aubergines and keep them warm in a low oven or reheat in the microwave when you're ready to serve.

Serves 4

GARLICKY GREENS WITH FERMENTED TOFU

RAU XÀO TỎI VỚI CHAO

Prep time 10 minutes
Cook time 6 minutes

- 1 tablespoon rapeseed (canola) oil
- 1 courgette (zucchini), sliced into rings
- 100 g (3½ oz) Tenderstem broccoli (broccolini)
- 4 garlic cloves, sliced
- 100 g (3½ oz) okra, stems removed and halved
- 100 g (3½ oz) fine green beans
- 1 tablespoon chilli (hot pepper) flakes or 1 fresh bird's eye chilli, finely chopped (optional)
- 1 tablespoon crispy chilli oil (optional)
- 1 tablespoon capers (optional)

FOR THE SAUCE

- 2 heaped teaspoons fermented tofu, mashed with 1 tablespoon water
- 2 tablespoons Yondu vegetable umami sauce or light soy sauce
- ½ teaspoon brown sugar
- 1 tablespoon cider vinegar

Fermented tofu has a deeply umami, funky and savoury taste that adds incredible flavour to dishes. I love using it on vegan days or when I have run out of fish sauce. It is available with a bit of chilli spice if you like that, too, which gives the many plants you can use in this simple stir-fry an extra magic kick. The cubes of fermented tofu can also be enjoyed sparingly on steamed rice.

First, make the sauce by mixing together all the ingredients in a bowl.

Heat the oil in a wok or frying pan over a medium-high heat, then add the courgette and Tenderstem broccoli. Stir-fry for 2 minutes until starting to char, then add the garlic. Stir-fry for a further minute, then add the okra and green beans. Pour over the sauce and cook for a further 2 minutes. Add the chilli flakes or fresh chilli and crispy chilli oil and capers, if using, then serve immediately.

Serves 4

VEGETARIAN FUJIAN-STYLE RICE

CƠM PHÚC KIẾN CHAY

Prep time 15 minutes
Cook time 25 minutes

To go the extra mile in a feast, embellish this rice dish with any seasonal vegetables you have growing or going. Frozen vegetables also work fantastically. Push your plant intake to the max. Otherwise, serve it as a midweek supper with leftovers on the side.

- 200 g (7 oz/1 cup) jasmine rice, washed three times
- 550 ml (18½ fl oz/generous 2⅓ cups) water
- ½ teaspoon sea salt, plus extra as needed
- ¾ teaspoon sesame oil
- 50 g (1¾ oz) carrot, cut into 1 cm (½ inch) cubes
- 50 g (1¾ oz) potato, cut into 1 cm (½ inch) cubes
- 50 g (1¾ oz) baby courgette (zucchini), cut into 1 cm (½ inch) cubes
- 50 g (1¾ oz) asparagus, cut into 1 cm (½ inch) lengths
- 50 g (1¾ oz/⅓ cup) fresh or frozen peas
- 1 tablespoon rapeseed (canola) oil
- 1 round shallot, sliced
- 2 garlic cloves, roughly chopped
- 1 tablespoon light soy sauce
- 1 tablespoon mushroom vegetarian stir-fry sauce
- ¾ tablespoon caster (superfine) sugar
- 1 tablespoon cornflour (cornstarch)
- freshly ground black pepper
- zest and juice of ¼ lemon
- 1 teaspoon toasted sesame seeds
- sprig of Thai basil
- lemon wedges, to serve

Cook the rice in a rice cooker or put the rice into a saucepan and add 400 ml (14 fl oz/generous 1½ cups) of the water, salt and ¼ teaspoon of the sesame oil. Cook, covered, over a medium heat for 5 minutes until the water has mostly been absorbed by the rice, then reduce the heat to low and cook for a further 15–18 minutes until fluffy. Remove from the heat, fluff up the rice and keep covered for a further 10 minutes.

Meanwhile, bring a saucepan of water to the boil and add the carrot and potato. Cook for 3 minutes, then add the courgette, asparagus and peas and cook for a further 2 minutes. Drain and set aside.

Heat the rapeseed oil in a frying pan over a medium heat and brown the shallot for 5 minutes, then add the garlic. Once the garlic starts to colour, add the drained vegetables, soy sauce, mushroom sauce, the remaining sesame oil and the sugar. Stir-fry for 5 minutes.

In a small bowl, combine the cornflour with the remaining 150 ml (5 fl oz/scant ⅔ cup) of water and a pinch of salt. Stir until there are no more lumps, then pour over the vegetables and cook for a couple of minutes until you have a thickened sauce.

To serve, place the rice on a platter and pour the vegetable mixture over the top. Season with black pepper, a squeeze of lemon and a sprinkle of zest, then top with the toasted sesame seeds and Thai basil.

3 WHOLESOME SOUPS

WHOLESOME SOUPS

Like many who fled Vietnam during the exodus that followed the war, my father braved the seas and made it to the UK. I remember my mother scrabbling for rice and packing a small case of dried fish and preserved ham when we initially tried to escape together, but we had to stay behind and he went on alone. Three years later, my dad bought us over as refugees, and my mum, my brother and I had the privilege of flying on our first flight to freedom. Along with a few framed pictures of Mary, Jesus and St Patrick, all embedded with crushed pearls and shells, she packed a woven box on wheels with cable-knitted jumpers, a final bag of rice (we thought we would be living on potatoes for the rest of our lives) and a bottle of fish sauce.

We enjoyed time with my father for a little while, sharing feasts and many family-style meals, but his heart was elsewhere. He had fallen in love with someone else on the boat over. He left. He began a new life and a new family and we didn't really see him again. Through the many family dramas that befell our little Vietnamese family in London, the thing that held us together was the comfort of beautiful Vietnamese broths. They had the ability to bring us a sense of love and gratitude despite it all. We had been rescued from mass famine, we were homed, safe and far from the fierce dangers that Vietnam represented at the time, and food of our country never left us.

My estranged father passed away during the writing of this book. It affected me deeply. It felt like a further termination – being left all over again; this time for real. When I came back from his funeral (a long and complicated trip to Louisiana, USA), the first thing I did was make a batch of fresh noodles and a Chicken Noodle Broth (page 83). I took consolation in sinking my hands into the dough, kneading away my heartache and trying to make sense of my pain. I quietly ate the soothing chicken soup and imagined him as he once was: young, loving and kind. He would have certainly enjoyed it, too, if he were there.

At the time and forever since, I took sanctuary with my childhood friend, Agnieszka, who was also a refugee, from Poland. We met when we were six years old at primary school and were inseparable. We hoovered over bowls of steaming hot noodle soups together. She was my refuge from a broken heart. She still slurps with delight when she eats my noodle soups. I love her for it because I know she can feel every ounce of love and effort that is poured into the bowl. When we went to Vietnam together, she searched for her own childhood taste of *phở* that she had tried from my mother. Soups and broths are dishes rich with memories, which make us remember to enjoy every minute, and every bite.

Serves 4

Prep time 45 minutes
Cook time 20 minutes

60 g (2 oz) lemongrass
1.5 litres (50 fl oz/6¼ cups) water
4 small round shallots, halved and charred in a hot, dry pan
1 chicken or beef stock cube
10 g (½ oz) palm sugar
2 garlic cloves, finely chopped
500 g (1 lb 2 oz) bavette (flank) or rump steak, thinly sliced
2 teaspoons shrimp paste
3 tablespoons premium fish sauce
2 tablespoons olive oil
2 teaspoons brown sugar
1 teaspoon chilli powder (optional)
320 g (11¼ oz) 1.2 mm rice vermicelli
50 g (1¾ oz) beansprouts
4 spring onions (scallions), sliced lengthways
20 g (¾ oz) coriander leaves
20 g (¾ oz) Vietnamese coriander (cilantro) leaves (optional)
1 small red onion, thinly sliced (optional)

TO SERVE

1 lime, quartered
2 bird's eye chillies, sliced
chilli oil (optional)

QUICK BÚN BÒ HUẾ

BÚN BÒ HUẾ - CÁCH NẤU NHANH

When I first met my cousin and soul sister, Thuý, as an adult in Phan Thiết, I asked if she knew how to make our grandma's famous lemongrass-scented beef noodle soup from Huế in Central Vietnam. Legend has it that it was a soup created for kings and queens of dynasties dating back to the 16th century, traditionally filled with an array of trimmings, herbs, plants, different cuts of pork, beef, fishcakes and tofu. Thuý said she didn't know our grandma's recipe – there were too many guarded secrets. Instead, Thuý has always made it in this super-fast way. Of course, sometimes you do want the bone broth that's been simmered for hours and all the trimmings, but most of the time the days call for something quick and easy to quench craving and this equally fulfilling version will definitely do.

Cut two-thirds of the lemongrass stalks in half, then slice the thicker halves in half again, lengthways. Char these parts over an open flame until the edges darken or in a dry frying pan for 3 minutes. Finely chop the thinner ends and set aside.

Pour the water into a saucepan, cover and bring to the boil. Add the charred shallots, stock cube, palm sugar and charred lemongrass. Remove from the heat and set aside to infuse.

Meanwhile, put the chopped lemongrass and garlic into a large bowl. Add 300 g (10½ oz) of the steak along with the shrimp paste, fish sauce, oil, brown sugar and chilli powder, if using. Mix well and set aside.

Bring a large saucepan of water to the boil and cook the noodles according to the packet instructions, then drain and rinse under hot water. Cover and set aside to dry.

Divide the beansprouts between bowls, then add the noodles, spring onions, herbs and red onion (if using) on one side. Place the remaining raw sliced steak on the other side.

Bring the broth back to a simmer, add the remaining lemongrass and cover.

Place a wok or large frying pan over a high heat. Scatter the marinated steak into the wok and fry for 1–2 minutes, tossing every 20 seconds, then transfer everything to the broth. Bring the broth to the boil. Ladle the meat into the bowls and top with more broth.

Serve steaming hot with the lime wedges, chillies and chilli oil, if using.

Serves 6

QUICK BEEF PHỞ

PHỞ BÒ - CÁCH NẤU NHANH

Prep time 25 minutes
Cook time 1¾ hours

- 400 g (1 lb) beef off-cuts, trimmings and fat, such as oxtail, shin or bavette (flank)
- 5 small round shallots or 1 large onion, halved
- 90 g (3¼ oz) fresh ginger root, peeled and halved
- 1.5 litres (50 fl oz/6¼ cups) water
- 8–10 star anise
- 10 g (½ oz) sea salt
- 10 g (½ oz) rock sugar
- 2 teaspoons mushroom seasoning powder
- 1 chicken or beef stock cube or beef phở stock cube
- 220 g (8 oz) flat rice noodles, soaked in boiling water for 3–5 minutes
- 40 g (1½ oz) coriander (cilantro) sprigs, sliced into 1 cm (½ inch) lengths
- 4 spring onions (scallions), sliced
- 30 g (1 oz) Thai basil leaves (optional)
- 300 g (10½ oz) beef steak, such as rib eye, sirloin or rump (optional)
- 3 tablespoons premium fish sauce
- 1 lemon or lime, quartered, to serve
- 1 bird's eye or red chilli, sliced, to serve

NOTE

Once everything is in the broth, this can transferred to a slow cooker and cooked for 2 hours, which will make the beef much more tender. If you're really pushed for time, just use a beef phở or beef stock cube and thin slices of rump steak. Place the raw steak in a bowl with noodles and whichever garnishes you like, then ladle over the hot stock – it should cook perfectly.

One thing I wish more than anything is that I could have *phở* on demand 24/7, but it's not possible unless you live in Sài Gòn (or Little Saigon in California). Ideally, beef phở should be simmered for a minimum of 3 hours so that the meat is just right, but luckily, it is possible to make a quick cheat's version.

Lots of flavour can be brewed from odd ends of beef and off-cuts from the butcher. Ask for free bones, too, but remember that so much flavour is in the flesh. If you only use bones, you'll be missing half the flavour. If time is of the essence, slice the meat really thinly and use thinly sliced steak when serving instead (see Notes, below). You can then continue to cook the meat in the leftover soup the next day.

Place the beef off-cuts into a bowl and cover with boiling water, then cover and set aside for 10 minutes, then drain.

Meanwhile, heat a large, dry saucepan over a high heat and char the shallots or onion and ginger on their flat sides until they become blackened on both sides. Add the water, cover and bring to the boil. Add the drained beef.

Lightly toast the star anise in a small, dry frying pan for a couple of minutes until fragrant, then add to the broth along with the salt, sugar, mushroom seasoning powder and stock cube.

Cover and simmer for 30 minutes or as long as you can, then remove from the heat and leave to infuse in the residual heat for a further 45 minutes.

Divide the noodles between bowls and add the coriander, spring onions and Thai basil, if using.

Remove the meat from the broth and thinly slice it, then place into the bowls. If using, thinly slice the raw steak into paper-thin strips and add raw to the bowls. Using a spider or skimmer, remove the star anise and any flakes of shallots and ginger from the broth and discard.

When ready to serve, bring the broth back to the boil, then add the fish sauce. Pour the broth over the noodles and serve with the lemon or lime wedges and chilli.

Serves 4

QUICK CHICKEN PHỞ

PHỞ GÀ - CÁCH NẤU NHANH

Prep time	15 minutes
Cook time	20 minutes

- 1.2 litres (40 fl oz/5 cups) chicken stock or water
- 1 onion, halved and charred in a hot, dry pan
- 40 g (1½ oz) fresh ginger root, peeled, halved and charred in a hot, dry pan
- 2 chicken or chicken phở stock cubes
- 20 g (¾ fl oz) rock sugar
- 3–5 star anise
- 2–3 tbsp premium fish sauce
- 320 g (11¼ oz) flat rice noodles, soaked in boiling water for 4–5 minutes
- 1 shop-bought rotisserie chicken, sliced (or use leftover roast chicken)
- 4 spring onions (scallions), sliced lengthways
- 40 g (1½ oz) coriander (cilantro) sprigs
- 20 g (¾ oz) Thai basil leaves
- freshly ground black pepper
- 1 lime, quartered, to serve

In Vietnamese supermarkets or online, you can buy stock cubes for making specific Vietnamese noodle soups, like the famous chicken or beef *phở*, the southern *hủ tiếu nam vang*, street-food favourite wonton noodle soup and midnight hawker's *miến gà*. Add to boiling water with a few additions like charred onion, ginger and star anise and you will have a quick and easy time creating some really delicious soups.

Pour the chicken stock or water into a saucepan and bring to the boil, then add the charred onion and ginger, stock cubes, rock sugar and star anise. Simmer for 10 minutes, then add the fish sauce, taste and adjust accordingly. Remove from the heat.

Divide the noodles between bowls, then add the sliced chicken, spring onions, coriander and Thai basil. Season with black pepper.

Bring the broth back up to the boil, then ladle over the noodles and serve with the lime wedges.

Serves 4

CHICKEN NOODLE SOUP WITH OMELETTE STRIPS AND FRIED SHALLOTS

BÁNH CANH GÀ TRỨNG

Prep time 40 minutes
Cook time 45 minutes–1 hour

1.2 litres (40 fl oz/5 cups) water
4 chicken legs or thighs and drumsticks
1 onion, peeled but left whole
½ tablespoon sea salt
1 chicken stock cube
20 g (¾ oz) rock sugar
1 tablespoon premium fish sauce
1 x quantity Homemade Thick-cut Noodles (page 214) or rice vermicelli

FOR THE OMELETTE

4 eggs (any size), beaten
pinch of sea salt
½ teaspoon brown sugar
1 spring onion (scallion), finely sliced
2 garlic cloves, finely chopped
1 tablespoon olive oil

TO GARNISH

handful of green vegetables, such as Tenderstem broccoli (broccolini) or Chinese mustard greens, steamed
20 g (¾ oz) coriander (cilantro) leaves, sliced
20 g (¾ oz) spring onions (scallions), sliced
4 heaped tablespoons Crispy Shallots (page 208, or use shop-bought)
1 lemon or lime, quartered

The great thing about using freshly cut, toothsome noodles is that they have great body, making this dish feel perfectly satisfying. If you can't make your own noodles, use udon, ramen noodles, rice noodles, vermicelli or glass noodles – it will be just as good.

Pour the water into a saucepan and bring to the boil, then add the chicken, onion, salt, stock cube and sugar. Reduce the heat to the lowest heat setting, cover and simmer for 20 minutes, then remove from the heat and let the residual heat do the rest of the cooking for 15 minutes.

To make the omelette, put the eggs, salt, sugar, spring onions and garlic into a bowl and whisk together for a couple of minutes until fluffy. Heat the oil in a frying pan over a medium heat and once it's nice and hot, then add the egg mixture. Use a spatula to gather the mixture from opposite sides to the middle of the pan, swirling it around, creating egg dunes. Let the beaten egg pour into the empty space to cook. Repeat around the pan until the egg is just cooked. Remove from the heat and when cool enough, slice the omelette into strips.

Remove the chicken from the broth and place in a bowl of cold water. Leave to rest for at least 5 minutes, then remove the chicken from the bones and slice against the grain.

Add the fish sauce to the broth, then taste and adjust the flavours as needed.

Divide the noodles between bowls, then add the chicken slices, omelette strips, vegetables, coriander, spring onions and crispy shallots.

Bring the broth back up to the boil, then ladle over the noodles and serve with the lemon or lime wedges.

NOTE

This is lovely with poached or boiled eggs, too, if you don't want to make an omelette.

Serves 4

Prep time 15 minutes
Cook time 40 minutes

- 1 litre (34 fl oz/4¼ cups) water
- 500 g (1 lb 2 oz) chicken thighs or drumsticks
- 1 chicken stock cube (optional)
- 30 g (1 oz) fresh ginger root, peeled and finely chopped
- 100 g (3½ oz) carrot, diced
- 250–300 g (9–10½ oz/1⅓–1⅔ cups) cooked rice
- ½ teaspoon ground turmeric
- 75 g (2½ oz) fine green beans, thinly sliced
- 2½ tablespoons premium fish sauce
- 15 g (½ oz) coriander (cilantro) leaves
- 1 lemon or lime, quartered
- freshly ground black pepper

OPTIONAL TOPPINGS

- Crispy Shallots (page 208, or use shop-bought)
- fresh ginger root, julienned
- crispy chilli oil
- watercress, rocket (arugula) or pea shoots

NOTE

If you don't have cooked rice, use about 100 g (3½ oz) of washed, uncooked rice and cook for a further 10 minutes.

GET-WELL-SOON CHICKEN RICE PORRIDGE

CHÁO GÀ KHỎE LẠI

When I am poorly or if my daughter is unwell, I immediately turn to the stove, just like my mother did. I will prepare a restorative rice porridge, full of the goodness of ginger, slivers of chicken or fish and herbs. Whether you're feeling under the weather or on top of the world, this comforting chicken rice soup will aid wellness and push you further. You can use absolutely any herbs and vegetables you have and it is so easy to cook, yet it has so much healing power. It is the best medicine for your body.

Pour the water into a saucepan and bring to the boil, then add the chicken thighs or drumsticks and stock cube, if using. Cover and simmer for 5 minutes, then add the ginger, carrot, rice and turmeric. Simmer, covered, for a further 25 minutes until the rice grains have blossomed and thickened the broth.

Remove the chicken pieces and separate the meat from the bones, then slice the meat.

Stir the green beans and fish sauce into the porridge and simmer for 5 minutes, then add the coriander. To serve, ladle into soup bowls and top with the sliced chicken and any additional toppings. Squeeze over the lemon or lime wedges and season with black pepper.

Serves 4–6

DUCK SALAD WITH RICE PORRIDGE

CHÁO VỊT BẮP CẢI

Prep time 45 minutes
Cook time 45 minutes

FOR THE RICE PORRIDGE

- 4 duck legs
- 1.2 litres (40 fl oz/5 cups) boiling water
- ½ tablespoon sea salt
- 6 g (¼ oz) rock sugar
- 1 teaspoon chicken or mushroom seasoning powder or 1 chicken stock cube
- 1 onion, halved and charred in a hot, dry pan
- 125 g (4½ oz/scant ⅔ cup) jasmine rice, washed three times
- 30 g (1 oz) fresh ginger root, peeled and finely chopped
- 1½ tablespoons premium fish sauce

FOR THE SALAD

- 2 tablespoons caster (superfine) sugar
- 2 tablespoons cider vinegar
- 2 teaspoons freshly ground black pepper, plus extra for the duck
- 50 g (1¾ oz) white cabbage, thinly sliced
- 50 g (1¾ oz) red cabbage, thinly sliced
- 50 g (1¾ oz) carrot, julienned
- 1 red onion, thinly sliced
- handful of Vietnamese coriander (cilantro) or coriander

FOR THE DIPPING SAUCE

- 10 g (½ oz) fresh ginger root, peeled and finely chopped or grated
- 2 bird's eye chillies, finely chopped
- zest of 1 lime, plus 2 tablespoons juice
- 3 tablespoons clear honey
- 4 tablespoons premium fish sauce

FOR THE FRIED SHALLOTS

- 2 tablespoons neutral oil
- 2 small round shallots, sliced

Though it might sound humble, this is usually served as a celebration dish, the whole duck presented alongside a blossoming rice porridge made from the duck's wholesome broth. To make a quicker version, this recipe uses duck legs. The textures here are brilliant together and the incredible flavours are truly comforting as well as vibrant. This meal reflects the true nature of Vietnamese cooking: sharing and nourishing. The sauce is not poured over the rice porridge, but rather used for dipping the salad. Use chicken if you don't want to use duck. It is utterly special.

Place the duck legs into a large saucepan and add the boiling water. Add the salt, rock sugar, chicken or mushroom powder or stock cube and the charred onion. Add the rice and ginger to the broth, then cover and bring to the boil, skimming off any foam. Cover and simmer for 25 minutes over a low heat until the rice grains have blossomed and thickened the broth. Stir in the fish sauce, then turn off the heat and let the residual heat cook the porridge for a further 20 minutes.

Once the duck has cooked, remove from the porridge and slice the meat or shred with forks.

Meanwhile, make the salad. Mix together the sugar, cider vinegar and black pepper in a small bowl to make a dressing. In a large bowl, combine the duck, cabbages, carrot and onion, then add the dressing and toss together. Add the coriander and toss again. Transfer to a serving platter and season with the black pepper.

To make the dipping sauce, mix together the ginger, chillies, lime zest and juice, honey and fish sauce in a bowl and then divide between individual dipping bowls.

Next, make the crispy shallots. Heat the oil in a small frying pan over a low heat and fry the shallots until golden and crispy, then transfer to a small bowl.

To serve, heat the porridge and ladle it into soup bowls. Place the duck salad, garnishes, fried shallots and more black pepper in the centre of the table for everyone to help themselves to.

Serves 4

WATERCRESS SOUP WITH FISH BALLS

CANH CÁ THÁC LÁC XÀ LÁCH XOONG

Prep time 15 minutes
Cook time 10 minutes

200 g (7 oz) skinless haddock, cod, coley or salmon fillets, finely chopped
1 small round shallot, diced
20 g (¾ oz) spring onions (scallions)
1 teaspoon ground black pepper
1 teaspoon caster (superfine) sugar
2½ tablespoons premium fish sauce
2 tablespoons olive oil
750 ml (25 fl oz/3 cups) hot chicken stock or water
20 g (¾ oz) fresh ginger root, peeled and sliced
100–200 g (3½–7 oz) watercress

Rice meals are always completed with a sharing soup that is set in the middle of the table for everyone to help themselves to. They can be dipped into at any point during the meal but are especially useful between rice servings to slurp up the leftover grains before the next round. The soup can also be added to half a bowl of rice, or the vegetables or fish balls can be picked out and enjoyed with a dipping sauce. Heaps of flavour seeps out of the watercress after it soaks in the hot broth, providing a soothing yet hugely invigorating taste along with the ginger.

Put the fish, shallot, spring onions, black pepper, sugar, 1 tablespoon of the fish sauce and 1 tablespoon of the oil into a bowl and whisk together using chopsticks.

Use the remaining olive oil to grease your hands and then divide the fish mixture into roughly 12 balls, about 3 cm (1¼ inches) in diameter. Set aside.

Pour the chicken stock or water into a saucepan, add the ginger and bring to a simmer. Add the fish balls and cook for 5 minutes until they float to the top, then add the watercress and season with the remaining fish sauce. Serve in individual rice bowls or a big serving bowl in the middle of the table for everyone to help themselves.

Serves 4

SUNSHINE SALMON, TOMATO, PINEAPPLE AND DILL SOUP

CANH CHUA CÁ HỒI

Prep time 10 minutes
Cook time 15 minutes

- 1 tablespoon vegetable oil
- 1 garlic clove, finely chopped
- 1 litre (34 fl oz/4¼ cups) boiling water
- 1 chicken stock cube
- 4 tomatoes, cut into quarters
- 1 x 230 g (8¼ oz) tin of pineapple chunks in juice, cut into bite-sized pieces
- 1 tablespoon brown sugar or 15 g (½ oz) rock sugar
- 50 g (1¾) beansprouts
- 100–200 g (3½–7 oz) skinless salmon fillet or steaks
- 2 tablespoons premium fish sauce
- zest and juice of 1 lime
- 30 g (1 oz) dill fronds or coriander (cilantro) leaves, sliced into 1 cm (½ inch) lengths, plus extra to serve
- 1 spring onion (scallion), sliced
- red or bird's eye chillies (optional), to serve

FOR THE DIPPING SAUCE

- 1–2 bird's eye chillies
- 1½ tablespoons premium fish sauce

NOTE

You can use any kind of fish for this soup and if you don't have pineapple, that's OK, just don't use it. It is also great with okra added 2 minutes before the end of cooking, sliced daikon and beetroot, rhubarb, taro root and any crunchy vegetables.

This sweet and sour soup is one of my favourites and will be on rotation in my house for as long as I shall live. It's usually a soup for sharing in the middle of the table and its ideal for those busy days as the soup and fish are both cooked in one pot, making two quick dishes in one. The fish is often transferred onto a plate of fish sauce and crushed chillies to be eaten with rice and the soup is enjoyed later on. This soup always restores my mind and nourishes me deeply. Serve with plenty of steamed rice.

Heat the oil in a saucepan over a medium heat and fry the garlic for 1 minute until golden, then pour the oil and garlic into a small bowl and set aside.

Pour the water into the same pan and add the stock cube, tomatoes, pineapple and its juice and sugar. Cover and bring to a simmer, then immediately add the beansprouts and salmon. Cover again and bring to the boil, then reduce to a simmer and cook for 3–5 minutes, until the fish is opaque and the beansprouts have wilted. Add the fish sauce and the lime juice, then taste and adjust the sweet, sour and salty balance as necessary. Remove from the heat, return the fried garlic to the pan, including their oil, then scatter in the dill or coriander and spring onion.

To serve, make the dipping sauce. Slice or crush the bird's eye chillies on a small plate with the back of a spoon, then add the fish sauce. Serve the soup in a large serving bowl in the middle of the table and garnish with the fresh chillies, if using, and extra herbs.

Serves 4

KIMCHI, TOFU AND TOMATO EGG DROP SOUP

CANH KIM CHI ĐẬU HŨ

Prep time 10 minutes
Cook time 15 minutes

- 1 litre (34 fl oz/4¼ cups) unseasoned chicken stock or water
- 1 chicken or vegetable stock cube
- 10 cherry tomatoes, halved
- 4 spring onions (scallions), sliced into 3 cm (1¼ inch) pieces
- 200–400 g (7–14 oz) medium-firm tofu, cut into 3 cm (1¼ inch) squares
- 2 eggs (any size), beaten
- 175 g (6 oz) kimchi (shop-bought or homemade, page 207), sliced
- 20 g (¾ oz) coriander (cilantro) leaves, roughly chopped
- vermicelli noodles, ramen noodles, steamed rice or crusty bread, to serve

A cross between *bún riêu* and Korean *jjigae*, this extremely quick and easy soup is delicious, nutritious and completely soothing and comforting on colder, rainy days. It can also serve as a canvas to enjoy lots of leftovers, as anything can be added to the mix, from whatever vegetables you have to roughly chopped meat or seafood. Add as little or as much tofu as you like, and feel free to add additional herbs or chillies if you want a little spice.

Pour the chicken stock or water into a saucepan and bring to the boil, then add the stock cube, cherry tomatoes, spring onions and tofu. Wait for it to come back up to a simmer, then use chopsticks or a spoon to swirl the soup. Gently pour in the beaten eggs while continuing to swirl. Cook for a further 2 minutes, then remove from the heat and add the kimchi and coriander.

To serve, either pour over vermicelli noodles, ramen noodles, steamed rice or eat as it is with crusty bread.

Serves 4

WINTER MELON SOUP WITH PORK BELLY AND CORIANDER

CANH BÍ ĐAU THỊT HEO

Prep time 5 minutes
Cook time 15 minutes

150 g (5½ oz) pork belly, sliced into 1 cm (½ inch) chunks
750 ml (25 fl oz/3 cups) hot water
40 g (1¼ oz) fresh ginger root, sliced
300 g (10½ oz) winter melon, peeled and thinly sliced
100 g (3½ oz) glass noodles, soaked in cold water for 10 minutes
2 tablespoons premium fish sauce
50 g (1¾ oz) coriander (cilantro) leaves, roughly chopped

Winter melon (also called wax gourd) is often sold in smaller cut pieces as it is a lengthy vegetable. The taste is delicious and floral and absolutely refreshing. It is great in soups as its flavour pours into the broth and its crunch contrasts with its softness, offering a pleasurable texture. Winter melon is one of my mum's favourite vegetables, as she claims that it is cooling for the body and mind.

Put the sliced pork belly into a bowl and cover with boiling water. Set aside for a few minutes, then drain.

Pour the hot water into a saucepan over a medium heat and add the pork belly, ginger and winter melon. Cover and simmer for 10–15 minutes until the pork is cooked through and the winter melon is soft, then add the noodles, fish sauce and coriander.

Serve in individual bowls or a large serving bowl in the middle of the table for everyone to help themselves.

NOTE

On meat-free days, leave out the pork belly and add fried or fresh tofu cubes. Use a vegetable stock cube and season with sea salt or nutritional yeast. You can substitute the winter melon for marrow, courgette (zucchini), pumpkin, watercress, spinach or Chinese mustard greens.

4 QUICK & EASY NOODLES

QUICK & EASY NOODLES

My friend Anja and I were film students at Central Saint Martins art college when, over hot lattes and takeaway (takeout) Singapore fried noodles, we decided to move to New York. Would anyone miss us if we took off for 6 months to learn from the school of life on the streets of Manhattan? There, we found an apartment, we filled it with furniture we found in skips, and lived off bagels and cream cheese. I desperately missed my mum's cooking and called her often for recipes. In our best British accents, we approached the many film crews we saw on the streets to ask if we could make coffee or English breakfast tea and help out where we could. Our story in New York worked out like a 1990s romcom, with heartache and happy endings. She married a cameraman, Beni, we met while there and they now have two grown children, Lavi and Leif – and one is my godson.

On one rare occasion when I was at home on a spring evening, I took a walk and found a small Vietnamese takeaway shop, brightly lit among the darkness between 1st Avenue and Avenue A. I leaped in there with joy, overwhelmed by choice and the possibility of all my favourite things. From a southern Vietnamese gentleman, I ordered *bún thịt nướng* (page 102), summer rolls (page 56), spring rolls and a chicken salad. I eagerly sped home to our tiny apartment on the first floor of a building on 4th Street, opened the tightly packed white lantern boxes decorated with red dragons and enjoyed one of the best meals of my entire life. I was in sheer bliss – and I missed my mum more than ever. The noodles were bouncy and fluffy with the right bite and consistency and the salad that came with them had all the right balance of herbs. The meat so sweet and succulent. I told myself I would never forget that moment – and I haven't. Happiness appeared to me and it wasn't in the form of love from any person, but rather the love and enjoyment of my kind of food.

Other types of noodles have influenced my life, too. I have been known to judge a person by their love of spaghetti vongole, and this chapter includes my Vietnamese version (page 108). It is such a fun and hands-on meal – you need to suck at the shells and slurp the noodles to fully enjoy it.

Most of the time, though, the noodles I eat are quick and easy lunches or dinner, pulling together whatever I have to hand to make a handsome meal. Recipes in this chapter are great to share with others but equally indulgent to eat alone.

Serves 2

CRISPY NOODLES WITH CALVES' LIVER AND VEGETABLES

MÌ XÀO GIÒN GAN BÊ

Prep time	15 minutes, plus 1 hour soak time
Cook time	30 minutes

- 160 g (5¾ oz) fresh ramen noodles, left to dry out at room temperature for a few hours
- 200 g (7 oz) calves' liver, sliced into 1 cm (½ inch) thick strips
- 200 ml (7 fl oz/scant 1 cup) whole milk
- 6 tablespoons olive oil
- 1 tablespoon cornflour (cornstarch), mixed with 2 tablespoons water
- 200 ml (7 fl oz/scant 1 cup) coconut water or chicken, beef or vegetable stock
- 2 small round shallots, sliced
- 2 garlic cloves, sliced
- 100 g (3½ oz) Tenderstem broccoli (broccolini), cut into bite-sized pieces on the diagonal
- 50 g (1¾ oz) baby corn, quartered lengthways
- 50 g (1¾ oz) carrot, peeled into ribbons
- 150 g (5 oz) Chinese broccoli (kai lan) leaves, sliced (optional)
- 50 g (1¾ oz) spring onions (scallions), sliced lengthways
- 1 mild red chilli, sliced
- freshly ground black pepper

FOR THE MARINADE

- 1 tablespoon premium fish sauce
- 1 tablespoon oyster sauce
- 1 tablespoon brown sugar
- ½ tablespoon cider vinegar
- 1 teaspoon sesame oil

These noodles scream Friday nights! When my mother found love for a second time, with my stepfather, Chú Tùng, I saw how much he loved watching her eat these crispy noodles – a recipe for love. He varied the ingredients, using beef, liver, ox tongue, seafood, vegetables and sometimes all of those mixed together. It was utterly delicious. Vary your ingredients every Friday night!

Bring a large saucepan of water to the boil and cook the noodles for about 2 minutes until they are half-cooked. Drain and rinse with warm water, then set aside to dry.

Put the calves' liver into a bowl and cover with the milk, and set aside to soak for 1 hour.

Heat the 6 tablespoons of olive oil in a wok or frying pan over a medium-high heat for 2–3 minutes. Add half the noodles and use chopsticks to spread them out to cover the pan. Let them crisp up for 1–2 minutes, then use a spatula to flip them over and cook for another 1–2 minutes until golden. Remove from the pan, drain on paper towels, then transfer to a plate. Repeat with the rest of the noodles.

Mix together all the ingredients for the marinade in a small bowl. Drain the calves' liver, then put the liver back into the bowl and add the marinade, mixing thoroughly.

Add the cornflour mix to the coconut water or stock.

Heat another tablespoon of the oil in a wok or large frying pan over a high heat and add the liver, reserving any leftover marinade for later. Sear for 1 minute on each side, then remove from the pan.

Add the remaining oil to the pan and fry the shallots and garlic for about 5 minutes until golden. Add the broccoli, baby corn and carrot and stir-fry for 30 seconds, then add the coconut water or stock mixture followed by the Chinese broccoli leaves, if using. Stir-fry until the leaves have almost wilted, then return the liver to the pan and pour over the reserved marinade. Stir-fry for 3 minutes - the vegetables should be releasing their juices and the sauce should be sizzling, thickening and reducing. Add the spring onions and chilli and cook for a further minute.

Dish up the stir-fry on top of the crispy noodles, pouring the gravy over the middle. Season with black pepper.

LEMONGRASS MEAT SKEWERS

BÚN THỊT NƯỚNG

Serves 4–5

Prep time	20 minutes, plus 1 hour marinating time
Cook time	17 minutes

- 4 small round shallots, finely diced
- 6 garlic cloves, finely chopped
- 50 g (1¾ oz) lemongrass, finely chopped
- 40 g (1½ oz/scant 14 cup) brown sugar or maple syrup
- 2 tablespoons premium fish sauce
- ½ tablespoon ground black pepper
- 3 tablespoons olive oil
- 650 g (1 lb 7 oz) pork belly, very thinly sliced, or chicken thighs, cut into bite-sized chunks
- Vermicelli Noodle Salad Bowls (page 210), to serve
- salad and pickles, to serve

FOR BASTING

- 1 tablespoon clear honey
- 1 tablespoon premium fish sauce

I often crave this street-food treat. The whole city of Sài Gòn is filled with the smoky vapours of lemongrass chicken or pork skewers sizzling and hissing over charcoal fires. I love their sultry, velvety texture served with vermicelli noodles, fresh leaves and zingy pickles. To me, this represents so much of what Vietnamese food is all about. It is heaven and earth, yin and yang, a balance of opposites. Make this as elaborate or as simple as you wish.

Put the shallots, garlic, lemongrass, sugar or maple syrup, fish sauce, pepper and oil into a bowl and whisk together until the sugar has dissolved.

Add the pork or chicken and stir to coat in the marinade, then cover and set aside to marinate for at least 1 hour, or overnight in the refrigerator.

Preheat the oven to 200°C fan (425°F).

Thread the marinated pork or chicken pieces onto soaked wooden or metal skewers and place on a wire rack set over a roasting tin. Cook in the oven for 12 minutes.

Meanwhile, mix together the honey and fish sauce in a small bowl.

Remove the pork or chicken from the oven and set the grill (broiler) to high. Brush the basting mixture over the skewers, then cook under the hot grill for 5 minutes, turning occasionally.

Serve with the vermicelli noodles, salad and pickles. It is also fantastic with added spring rolls (page 163) for a real treat.

NOTE

If using pork belly, freeze it for 1 hour to make it easier to slice.

Serves 2

Prep time 20 minutes
Cook time 20 minutes

- 160 g (5¾ oz) 0.8 mm rice vermicelli (2 nests)
- ¾ tablespoon brown sugar
- 1½ tablespoons premium fish sauce
- 1 tablespoon olive oil
- 1 small onion, diced
- 15 g (½ oz) lemongrass, stalk halved and bashed
- 2 garlic cloves, roughly chopped
- 60 g (2 oz) daikon, quartered and thinly sliced
- 250 g (9 oz) minced (ground) pork
- 4 spring onions (scallions), sliced
- 20 g (¾ oz) Thai basil leaves
- juice of ½ lime
- pickles, ferments and steamed vegetables, to serve (optional)

NOTE

If you can't find Thai basil, use coriander (cilantro) instead. This is also great with fresh ginger if you don't have lemongrass. Use regular radishes if you can't get daikon. You can also use ground (minced) chicken.

LEMONGRASS MINCED PORK VERMICELLI

BÚN THỊT BẰM XÀO SẢ

Quick, easy and delightful, the pork is also lovely on steamed rice, in lettuce cups or as a noodle salad bowl with something pickled and fermented and an array of herbs and leaves. Do as much or as little as desired.

Put the noodles into a bowl and cover with boiling water, then set aside to soak for 10 minutes. Drain, then leave in the colander, covered, for 10 minutes to dry and fluff up.

Mix together the sugar and fish sauce in a small bowl and set aside.

Heat the oil in a frying pan over a medium heat and brown the onions and lemongrass for 5 minutes. Add the garlic and fry for a couple of minutes, then add the daikon. Stir for 1 minute, then add the pork and use a spatula to spread out and break up the meat.

Add the sugar and fish sauce mixture and stir-fry for 3–5 minutes until cooked through, then throw in the spring onions. The green is such a delightful sight! Cook for a further 2 minutes, then remove from the heat, add the Thai basil and fold together.

To serve, divide the noodles between bowls and scoop the minced pork over the noodles. Squeeze over the lime juice. Serve with pickles, ferments and any steamed vegetables you like.

Serves 4

BAKED MARMALADE CHICKEN THIGHS WITH SPRING ONION NOODLES

MÌ GÀ NƯỚNG

Prep time 10 minutes
Cook time 40 minutes

- 600 g (1 lb 5 oz) chicken thighs, skin left on
- 2 tablespoons marmalade, mashed with a fork
- 4 tablespoons premium fish sauce or light soy sauce
- 1–2 tablespoons chilli (hot pepper) flakes (optional)
- 300 ml (10 fl oz/1¼ cups) coconut water
- 1 tablespoon salted butter
- 6 garlic cloves, peeled and smashed
- 30 g (1 oz) fresh ginger root, sliced
- zest and juice of 1 lime
- 2 teaspoons sesame oil
- 1 red chilli, sliced (optional)

FOR THE NOODLES

- 200 g (7 oz) medium egg noodles or ramen noodles
- 2 tablespoons olive oil
- 1 tablespoon salted butter
- 4–8 spring onions (scallions), sliced lengthways

Midweek dinners can be the best. I love simplicity, and here I use the chicken roasting juices to coat the noodles or pasta. Always save these juices so that you can stir them into a quick noodle lunch, use them as a dipping sauce or add them to a marinade.

Preheat the oven to 180°C fan (400°F).

Place the chicken thighs into a baking tray (pan), skin side up.

In a small bowl, mix together the marmalade and fish or soy sauce with the chilli flakes, if using. Pour this evenly over the chicken, using a pastry brush or the back of a spoon to coat the pieces. Pour the coconut water into the tray (not over the chicken). Bake in the oven for 35 minutes, basting halfway through.

Melt the butter in a small saucepan over a medium heat and add the garlic and ginger. Cook for 2 minutes, then set aside. Pour the butter over the chicken 5 minutes before the end of the cooking time.

Meanwhile, bring a large saucepan of water to the boil and cook the noodles according to the packet instructions, draining when they still have a good bite. Rinse under lukewarm water, then drain and toss with the olive oil to prevent them from sticking.

When the chicken is done, remove from the oven and allow to rest for 5–10 minutes, then transfer to serving plates, leaving the roasting juices in the pan.

Heat the butter in a small saucepan over a medium heat and add the spring onions. Cook for 1 minute, stirring to prevent them from burning, then add them to the roasting juices in the roasting pan. Add the noodles and toss well until all the noodles are coated in the juices.

Serve the noodles with the chicken thighs and finish with the lime zest and juice, sesame oil and chilli, if using.

Serves 2 or 4 as a starter

Prep time 15 minutes
Cook time 10 minutes

2 tablespoons olive oil
30 g (1 oz) lemongrass stalks, halved and bashed
4 garlic cloves, sliced
6 bird's eye chillies, 4 left whole and 2 sliced
1 kg (2 lb 2 oz) fresh clams
100 ml (3½ fl oz/scant ½ cup) coconut water or white wine
2 tablespoons premium fish sauce
100 g (3½ oz) glass noodles, soaked in cold water for 10 minutes
4 spring onions (scallions), sliced lengthways
30 g (1 oz) Vietnamese coriander (cilantro) leaves, Thai basil leaves, coriander (cilantro) leaves or Thai parsley leaves, roughly torn, plus extra to serve
zest and juice of 1 lime or lemon

GLASS NOODLES WITH CLAMS

MIẾN XÀO NGHÊU

Spaghetti vongole is one of my all-time favourite dishes. I would happily live in Italy eating this in all the months with an 'R'! Here is my own lovely Vietnamese version. I use glass noodles because they soak up all the delicious juices and they are fine and delicate just like the clams. It is equally delicious with fatter vermicelli noodles that mimic the texture of spaghetti, though. If you want to use these, cook the vermicelli first and then fold through the cooked clams at the end.

Heat the oil in a wok or large frying pan with a lid over a medium-high heat, then add the lemongrass, garlic and whole chillies. Toss until the garlic turns golden, then add the clams and increase the heat to high. Let them sit for a minute, then add the coconut water or wine, fish sauce and glass noodles. Combine vigorously, then add the spring onions and herbs. Toss or stir everything together, then cover with a lid and cook for 3–5 minutes, shaking the pan occasionally, until all the clams have opened and the noodles are transparent.

Discard any closed clams, then transfer everything to a serving platter or plates and finish with the lime or lemon zest and juice. Top with some extra herbs and the sliced chillies.

Serves 2

Prep time 10 minutes
Cook time 15 minutes

FOR THE OMELETTE MIX

- 2 large eggs
- 1 teaspoon fermented tofu, mashed, or 1 teaspoon premium fish sauce
- ¼ teaspoon sea salt
- 1 teaspoon chilli (hot pepper) flakes (optional)

FOR THE NOODLES

- 2 tablespoons olive oil
- 2 small round shallots, sliced
- 3 garlic cloves, sliced
- 50 g (1¾ oz) runner beans, cut into 10 cm (4 inch) lengths
- 1 leaf of Chinese (napa) cabbage, sliced into a 1 cm (½ inch) thick piece
- 200 g (7 oz) fresh flat rice noodles, separated into individual strands
- 1 tablespoon oyster sauce
- 1 tablespoon light soy sauce
- 1 teaspoon tamarind sauce (not paste)

TO SERVE

- lime wedges
- coriander (cilantro) leaves, Thai basil leaves or garlic chives, roughly torn

FRIED RICE-NOODLE OMELETTE

BÁNH PHỞ CHIÊN TRỨNG

This is a great communal dish to share. When served, someone should separate the omelette into rough portions so that it is easier for everyone to help themselves to a piece. Feel free to use any other crunchy greens you have.

Whisk together the omelette ingredients in a bowl and set aside.

For the noodles, heat half the oil in a large frying pan over a medium-high heat and fry the shallots for 5 minutes until they start to colour. Add the garlic and cook for 2 minutes until it starts to colour, then add the runner beans and cabbage. Fry for a minute until the leaves have wilted. Set the vegetables aside on a plate.

Add the rest of the olive oil to the wok and increase the heat to high, then add the noodles, oyster sauce, soy sauce and tamarind sauce. Let the noodles sit for a minute to char, then use a thin, flat spatula to gently toss and fold the noodles over in the sauce. Let the noodles sit again and then repeat until all the noodles get a turn on the bottom or edges of the wok. Return the vegetables to the wok and stir though.

Add the omelette mix and let it sit for 3–5 minutes to cook. Once done, slide the omelette onto a platter. The egg should still be cooking through at this point.

Serve immediately with a squeeze of lime and herb garnishes of your choice.

Serves 2

EASY CHINESE CABBAGE NOODLES

MÌ XÀO CẢI THẢO

Prep time 5 minutes
Cook time 15 minutes

120 g (4¼ oz) fine egg noodles (2 nests)
2 tablespoons olive oil
2 small round shallots, sliced lengthways into six
2 garlic cloves, sliced
5 g (¼ oz) fresh ginger root, peeled and grated
2 leaves of Chinese (napa) cabbage, sliced into 1 cm (½ inch) thick strips
1 tablespoon light soy sauce
½ tablespoon oyster sauce
1 tablespoon chilli oil (optional)

When making fried noodles, it's best to fry them in batches of two portions unless you have a very large frying pan or wok. Cooking them in smaller amounts allows you to properly mix the ingredients together without anything burning or some parts getting soggy. If serving more than two people, simply scale up the recipe in batches. I love these noodles with a fried fillet of fish or topped with crispy tofu. You can use any sliced greens, even just a bunch of spring onions (scallions) or garlic chives.

Bring a large saucepan of water to the boil and cook the noodles according to the packet instructions, minus 2 minutes cooking time. Drain and rinse in warm water to remove any excess starch. Toss the noodles with ½ tablespoon of the oil to prevent them from sticking together, then set aside.

Heat the remaining oil in a wok or frying pan over a medium-high heat and fry the shallots, garlic and ginger for 2 minutes until starting to brown, then add the cabbage, soy sauce and oyster sauce. Stir-fry for a couple of minutes until the leaves have wilted, then add the noodles. Use cooking chopsticks to move the noodles around and toss them with the vegetables. Stir-fry for a couple more minutes until hot and well combined, then serve immediately with or without chilli oil.

Serves 2

SPINACH NOODLES WITH AUBERGINE AND SPRING GREENS

MÌ RAU CỦ XÀO CÀ TÍM VÀ RAU

Prep time 5 minutes
Cook time 20 minutes

- 2 handfuls (about 120 g/4½ oz) Spinach Noodles (page 212)
- 1 tablespoon olive oil
- 1 small round shallot, sliced
- 2 garlic cloves, sliced
- ½ aubergine (eggplant), quartered lengthways then cut into 5 mm (¼ inch) slices
- 1 tablespoon premium fish sauce
- 1 tablespoon mirin
- 50 ml (1¾ fl oz/3½ tablespoons) coconut water or water
- 2 leaves of spring (collard) greens, sliced into ribbons
- 1 tablespoon oyster sauce
- 1 teaspoon chilli powder or flakes (optional)

Time permitting, I love making fresh spinach noodles. However, you can also buy noodles made with plants, so please use those instead for this recipe if you are time poor. I really enjoy eating my greens and usually pack my noodle dishes with plenty of them. Substitute the spring (collard) greens for cabbage, courgettes (zucchini), fine green beans or a bunch of coriander (cilantro) if you prefer. This is also great topped with leftover proteins or a fried egg.

Bring a large saucepan of water to the boil and cook the noodles according to the packet instructions, minus 2 minutes cooking time, then drain, rinse and set aside.

Heat the oil in a wok or frying pan over a medium-high heat and fry the shallot for about 2 minutes until golden, then add the garlic. Let the garlic colour briefly, stirring to flavour the oil. Add the aubergine and fry for a couple of minutes.

Mix together the fish sauce and mirin in a small bowl, then pour it around the wok and stir-fry vigorously for a couple of minutes so that everything soaks up the sauce. When the wok becomes dry, add the coconut water or water and let it sizzle. Add the spring greens and stir-fry for about 2 minutes until wilted.

Finally, add the noodles and oyster sauce and stir-fry for a further 2 minutes.

Sprinkle with chilli powder or flakes (if using) and serve immediately.

Serves 2

Prep time 5 minutes
Cook time 15 minutes

200 g (7 oz) pappardelle
knob of salted butter
4 garlic cloves, crushed
2 tablespoons chilli (hot pepper) flakes
2 tablespoons Crispy Shallots (page 208, or use shop-bought)
2 spring onions (scallions), sliced
1 tablespoon sesame seeds
2 tablespoons crispy chilli oil
1 tablespoon premium fish sauce
50 g (1¾ oz) coriander (cilantro), leaves and stalks, chopped
2 tablespoons rapeseed (canola) oil

CHILLI PAPPARDELLE

MÌ XÀO SA TẾ

This is a super-quick and easy dish to whip up and add to a lavish banquet. Or, if time is not an issue, it is a great recipe for those leisurely making-homemade-pasta sorts of afternoons. Flat rice noodles or torn lasagne sheets are also great with this if that's what you have.

Bring a large saucepan of water to the boil and cook the pappardelle according to the packet instructions, then drain and toss with the butter.

Put the garlic, chilli flakes, crispy shallots, spring onions, sesame seeds, crispy chilli oil, fish sauce and half the coriander onto a large heatproof serving platter or in a bowl.

Put the rapeseed oil into a small saucepan over a medium heat and heat until you can start to see steam. Remove from the heat and carefully pour over the ingredients on the platter. It should splutter and sizzle, so take care not to burn yourself.

Add the pappardelle and toss well together, then sprinkle with the remaining coriander. Serve immediately.

Serves 2

FRIED THICK-CUT NOODLES WITH VEGETABLES

BÁNH CANH XÀO RAU CỦ

Prep time 10 minutes
Cook time 15 minutes

400 g (14 oz) Homemade Thick-cut Noodles (page 214) or 2 x 200 g (7 oz) packets of fresh udon noodles
4½ tablespoons olive oil
1 tablespoon light soy sauce or premium fish sauce
1 tablespoon maple syrup
1 teaspoon cider vinegar
2 small round shallots, sliced
1 tablespoon oyster sauce or ½ tablespoon black bean sauce
pinch of freshly ground black pepper
4 garlic cloves, finely chopped
50 g (1¾ oz) sprouting broccoli, cut into bite-sized pieces
50 g (1¾ oz) fine green beans, cut into bite-sized pieces
50 g (1¾ oz) fennel, shaved
50 ml (1¾ fl oz/3½ tablespoons) water
50 g (1¾ oz) beansprouts
1 red chilli, sliced (optional)

These homemade noodles are a pure delight when fried as the edges char and take on colour and flavour. It's a great dish to impress guests and a gorgeous vessel for seasonal vegetables. Everybody will love the simplicity of the flavours and textures in this dish, with crunchy vegetables and toothsome noodles.

Bring a large saucepan of water to the boil and cook the noodles for 3 minutes, then drain and rinse well. Toss the noodles with 1½ tablespoons of the oil to prevent them from sticking, then set aside.

In a small bowl, mix together the soy or fish sauce, maple syrup and cider vinegar and set aside.

Heat 2 tablespoons of the oil in a wok or large frying pan over a medium-high heat and fry the shallots for about 5 minutes until golden, then add the noodles. Let the noodles sit for a minute to char, then gently flip them with a thin, flat spatula to char the other side for a minute more. Drizzle the noodles with the oyster sauce and season with the black pepper. Stir-fry, taking care not to break the noodles, for 2–3 minutes, then set aside on a platter or divide between plates.

Add the remaining oil to the same pan and increase the heat to high. Add the garlic and as soon as it turns golden, add the broccoli, beans and fennel. Let it sit for 20 seconds, then splash in the water to steam the vegetables, add the soy sauce mixture and stir-fry for 2 minutes before adding the beansprouts and red chilli, if using. Stir-fry for another minute until the beansprouts have wilted a little. Remove from the heat and dish up on top of the noodles, weaving the stir-fry into the noodles with chopsticks. Serve immediately.

5 RICE

RICE

I used to travel to Vietnam often as I bought fabric and made clothes with a seamstress in Sài Gòn for my boutique, Leluu, in Central London. I would spend days at a time in the crowded, hot and humid fabric section in Bến Thành market. The women would eat rice with braised sardines on piles of neatly folded off-cuts – their trays always contained a separate bowl for winter melon soup, a dipping sauce and a ferment. Women ran around the narrow lanes selling iced sugar cane drinks to buyers and the smell of rice filled the fan-blown air.

My cousins, Thuý and Thảo, took great care of me when I was there. I love them dearly for all the times they cooked for me. They cook every day for their parents (who are now elderly), children and anyone else who might drop by. In the mornings, one would take a bamboo sun hat and walk to the market to buy a handful of coriander (cilantro), a couple tomatoes, a fish caught that morning and so on. In turn, they would effortlessly and rather quickly cook an array of dishes for the rice table. It might be Lemony Ginger Pork Belly with Chinese Cabbage (page 124) and Pan-fried Fish with Green Mango (page 138) followed by Sunshine Salmon Tomato, Pineapple and Dill Soup (page 90) and Garlicky Greens with Fermented Tofu (page 69). I would eat bowl after bowl of rice, picking at the dishes along with the entire family, young and old, who were seated around the table. A little protein went a long way, as it was eaten modestly with plenty of vegetables and a sour ferment or pickle. Having grown up during the post-war, peak-famine years of extreme political change, they made do with the little they had, but they always poured flavour into every meal for their loved ones.

Thuý and I sometimes went on trips around the southern coast to sun ourselves at beach resorts and explore local markets. There were great rice (ăn cơm) restaurants dotted along the bustling and dusty highways where they would bake rice in terracotta pots, the vessel broken open to access the gorgeously cooked grains. We weren't always lucky with what we picked, though, and on the occasions where we could not handle another bad meal from a restaurant, we would order steamed rice from room service and top it with a tin of tuna or sardines, purchased earlier as an emergency. Thuý would slice a cucumber and crack open a bottle of Maggi seasoning and we would eat watching the sunset, drinking lukewarm cans of beer poured into hotel cups of ice. We often ate in comfortable silence, only uttering a word once we were almost full. Thuý is the only person who clearly understands all my sentiments spoken in broken, childlike Vietnamese.

Times have changed in Vietnam since I first discovered my soul sisters in 2000. They witnessed one of the fastest economic and cultural growths but when it comes down to it, everybody likes to eat rice.

Serves 4

LEMONY GINGER PORK BELLY WITH CHINESE CABBAGE

THỊT BA RỌI XÀO CẢI

Prep time 15 minutes
Cook time 1 hour

- 600 g (1 lb 5 oz) pork belly, sliced into bite-sized pieces, with or without fat
- 1 tablespoon lemon curd
- 1 teaspoon sea salt
- 1 teaspoon ground white pepper
- 1 tablespoon cornflour (cornstarch)
- 1 tablespoon olive oil
- 2 shallots, sliced
- 1 onion, quartered
- 4 garlic cloves, sliced
- 30 g (1 oz) fresh ginger root, peeled and sliced
- 100 ml (3½ fl oz/scant ½ cup) coconut water
- 1½ tablespoons premium fish sauce
- 100 g (3½ oz/scant ½ cup) chestnut (cremini) mushrooms, thinly sliced
- 400 g (14 oz) Chinese (napa) cabbage, sliced into 1 cm (½ inch) thick pieces
- 4 spring onions (scallions), cut into 3 cm (1¼ inch) lengths
- steamed jasmine rice, to serve
- juice of ¼ lemon, to serve

The word *kho* in Vietnamese means to braise or slow-cook. For typical Vietnamese dinners this is usually done in one pot. To *kho* quicker, slice the pork thinner (about 1 cm/½ inch pieces). I love pork fat, so here I have chosen to use belly as it has layers upon layers of fat for maximum flavour, but you can also use a leaner cut if you prefer. Alternatively, this is great with chicken thighs. If you want to prepare this ahead of time, cook the dish and then add the cabbage just before you're ready to serve so the leaves still have a fresh crunch (although once wilted and reheated it is also incredibly delicious). I love to cook slightly more of this so that I have leftovers – it is extremely addictive with steamed rice, homemade pickles or ferments and additional steamed vegetables.

Put the pork belly into a bowl and coat with the lemon curd, sea salt and white pepper, then toss in the cornflour.

Heat the oil in a frying pan over a medium-low heat, then add the shallots, onion, garlic and ginger.

Let the shallots brown for 3–5 minutes, then add half the pork belly slices. Cook for 5 minutes without turning to brown the slices, then flip and repeat on the other side. Once browned, move them to the side of the pan (or onto a plate) and brown the rest of the pork. Stir everything together, then cover and cook for 15–20 minutes, stirring occasionally, until caramelised.

Add the coconut water and fish sauce, then throw in the mushrooms and cabbage. Cook for 10 minutes, then add the spring onions. Cook for a further 10 minutes, or more if you like the texture of the belly to be softer.

Serve with steamed jasmine rice and a squeeze of lemon.

Serves 4

Prep time 10 minutes, plus 2 hours or overnight marinating time
Cook time 30 minutes

2 pork chops, sliced into 1 cm (½ inch) thick pieces, leaving the fat on at one end if desired (I do)
2 tablespoons extra virgin olive oil
2 tablespoons premium fish sauce
150 g (5½ oz) cavolo nero (lacinato kale) or kale, sliced into 4 cm (1½ inch) thick pieces
4 heaped tablespoons kimchi (shop-bought or homemade, page 207), sliced
freshly ground black pepper
steamed or sticky rice, to serve

FOR THE MARINADE

4 garlic cloves, roughly chopped
30 g (1 oz) lemongrass, finely chopped
2 small round shallots, thinly sliced
200 g (7 oz) fresh or tinned pineapple, plus its juices, mashed with a fork
1 teaspoon brown sugar or 2 teaspoons honey or marmalade
2 bird's eye chillies, deseeded and sliced (optional)
2 tablespoons premium fish sauce

NOTE

Keep the bones from your chops to make a simple soup, such as the Winter Melon Soup with Pork Belly and Coriander on page 95 to serve with this meal or freeze them for the future use.

SLICED PORK CHOP WITH KIMCHI AND LEMONGRASS

THỊT KHO SẢ KIM CHI

This is a great prep-ahead recipe; it reheats really well and tastes amazing. Cook for longer if you prefer a softer texture. It is also a good way to use less meat as it only needs two chops between four people. I've used my favourite ferment, kimchi, which is great for your gut microbiome, and cavolo nero (lacinato kale), because it has high levels of antioxidant polyphenols, but feel free to use sauerkraut and other dark or green leafy vegetables if you prefer. A big handful of torn coriander (cilantro) folded in at the last minute also works well and for extra delight, try topping it off with a fried egg and a generous seasoning of black pepper.

Combine all the ingredients for the marinade in an airtight container.

Add the pork chop slices, stir to coat evenly in the marinade and then transfer to the refrigerator to marinate for 2 hours or overnight.

When you're ready to cook, remove the pork from the refrigerator and let it to come to room temperature.

Heat the oil in a saucepan over a medium heat. Once hot, add half the pork and half the marinade and fry for 2 minutes before adding the rest to the pan. Cook for a further 15–20 minutes, then add the fish sauce and cavolo nero or kale. Stir the leaves into the mixture and let it wilt. Cook for a further 5 minutes, then fold in the kimchi. Let that warm through for a minute then remove from the heat and season with black pepper.

Serve immediately with steamed or sticky rice.

RICE-COOKER CHICKEN AND RICE

CƠM GÀ NỒI CƠM ĐIỆN

Serves 4

Prep time 15 minutes
Cook time 35–40 minutes

Making traditional Hainanese chicken and rice can be a long process, but on unfussy days, this simplified version is equally delicious. If you have a small rice cooker, use drumsticks or thighs instead of legs. There are lots of comfort foods that rank high on my favourites. This is one of them.

- 2 tablespoons chicken fat or olive oil
- 1 round shallot, roughly sliced
- 5 garlic cloves, peeled but left whole
- 300 g (10½ oz/1½ cups) jasmine rice, rinsed and drained
- 1 teaspoon mushroom or chicken seasoning powder
- 1 teaspoon sea salt
- 20 g (¾ oz) fresh ginger root, peeled and sliced
- 2 pandan leaves, tied in a knot (optional)
- 1 chicken stock cube
- 1 heaped teaspoon ground turmeric
- 500 ml (17 fl oz/generous 2 cups) boiling water
- 4 chicken legs (or drumsticks and thighs if you don't have space for legs)
- 1 teaspoon sesame oil

FOR THE DIPPING SAUCE

- 4 tablespoons light soy sauce or premium fish sauce
- 20 g (¾ oz) fresh ginger root, peeled and very finely chopped
- 1 tablespoon maple syrup
- 2 teaspoons sesame oil
- 1 tablespoon rice wine or cider vinegar
- 2 tablespoons hot chilli sauce (optional)

TO SERVE

- sliced tomatoes and cucumber or poached vegetables
- Spring Onion Oil (page 208; optional)

Heat the chicken fat or olive oil in a large frying pan over a medium heat and fry the shallot and garlic for a few minutes, then add the washed rice. Season with the mushroom or chicken powder and salt. Stir to combine, then transfer everything to a rice cooker along with the ginger and pandan leaves, if using. (If you're feeling really lazy, you don't even need to fry off the shallot and garlic, just add it to the rice cooker.)

Put the stock cube and turmeric into a jug (pitcher), then add the boiling water and stir to dissolve. Pour this into the rice cooker and place the chicken legs or pieces on top. Set the rice cooker to cook.

Meanwhile, make the dipping sauce by mixing together all the ingredients in a bowl. Transfer to individual bowls before serving.

When the rice cooker is done, let everything sit inside for a further 10 minutes, then remove the chicken legs. Brush the chicken with the sesame oil.

Use a rice paddle or fork to fluff up the rice and let it sit on the 'keep warm' setting.

Slice the chicken into bite-sized strips (or leave whole) and remove the bones, if desired. Serve with the rice, vegetables, spring onion oil, if using, and dipping sauce.

Serves 4

CHICKEN AND CAULIFLOWER CURRY

CƠM GÀ NỒI CƠM ĐIỆN

Prep time 15 minutes
Cook time 40 minutes

3 tablespoons extra virgin olive oil
2 small round shallots, sliced
50 g (1¾ oz) fresh ginger root, peeled and finely chopped
2 lemongrass (about 30 g/1 oz), finely chopped
4 garlic cloves, roughly chopped
500 g (1 lb 2 oz) boneless chicken thighs, cut into bite-sized pieces
2–3 heaped tablespoons Vietnamese curry powder
1–2 heaped tablespoons chilli (hot pepper) flakes, according to taste (optional)
500 g (1 lb 2 oz) cauliflower, cut into bite-sized florets
4 small carrots, quartered lengthways (optional)
400 ml (14 fl oz/generous 1½ cups) coconut cream or milk
200 ml (7 fl oz/scant 1 cup) coconut water or water
2 chicken stock cubes
100 g (3½ oz) cavolo nero (lacinato kale), sliced into 4 cm (1½ in) thick pieces
2 tablespoons premium fish sauce
20 g (¾ oz) coriander (cilantro) leaves, roughly sliced
1 lime, quartered, to serve
1 red chilli, sliced (optional), to serve
sprig of Thai basil (optional), to serve
steamed rice, crusty baguette or buttered toast, to serve

This is an easy, throw-it-all-in-the-pot recipe. If you want to prepare it earlier and serve it later on in the day, you can cook it for the first 20 minutes and then finish it off just before serving. Feel free to add more vegetables to the mix or leave out the chicken altogether. It is a very easy dish for using up what is available – just be mindful of texture and how the vegetables contrast with each other and add softer vegetables towards the end of cooking. The curry will continue to cook in its residual heat, too. Use a combination of ginger and lemongrass or one or the other.

Heat the oil in a large frying pan or casserole dish (Dutch oven) over a medium heat, then fry the shallots, ginger, lemongrass and garlic for a couple of minutes until they start to brown. Add the chicken pieces, sprinkle over the curry powder and chilli flakes, if using, then stir-fry together for about 5 minutes to get a good even coating on all the chicken pieces. Add the cauliflower and carrots, if using, and stir together.

Add the coconut cream or milk, coconut water and stock cubes. Stir well, then cook, covered, for 20 minutes over a medium-low heat, stirring occasionally. Add the cavolo nero and season with the fish sauce, then cook gently for a further 10 minutes.

Stir through the coriander, then serve with a squeeze of lime, the chilli and Thai basil, if using. Serve with steamed rice, crusty baguette or buttered toast.

NOTE

For an additional nutty and caramelised flavour, roast the cauliflower florets with a little salt (no oil) in a 200°C fan (425°F) oven for 25 minutes and then add to the curry for the last 10 minutes.

Serves 4

QUICK-BRAISED SALMON STEAKS WITH PALM SUGAR AND FISH SAUCE

CÁ KHO TỘ

Prep time 5 minutes
Cook time 20–25 minutes

- 2 tablespoons olive oil
- 30 g (1 oz) palm or rock sugar
- 2 small round shallots, sliced
- 500 g (1 lb 2 oz) salmon steaks or cod, hake or haddock fillets
- 3 tablespoons premium fish sauce
- 2 tablespoons coconut water or water
- 1 teaspoon freshly ground black pepper
- 4 bird's eye chillies
- steamed rice, vegetables and pickles and ferments, to serve

Here is a cheat's version of the much-loved Vietnamese dish, *cá kho*. This is the most simple and traditional version, which you can add to and layer with other flavours as you wish. If you have two spare lemongrass stalks, finely chop or halve and bash them and add those with the shallots, or likewise, a thumb-sized piece of fresh ginger root, julienned, will infuse nicely with the fish.

It's worthwhile investing in a flameproof clay pot for these easy braised dishes as they provide even heat distribution and extra deliciousness. If you don't have one, a small/medium deep frying pan or casserole dish (Dutch oven) with a lid does the trick. Don't forget to stick the rice on when you start so that everything is done at the same time.

Put the olive oil and palm or rock sugar into a clay pot over a medium heat. Wait for the sugar to melt and caramelise, then add the shallots. Wait until the shallots start to brown and crisp up (about 6–8 minutes), then add the salmon steaks. Pour in the fish sauce and coconut water or water. Using a spoon, cover the fish with the sugar, shallot and fish sauce juices. Season with the black pepper, then throw in the whole bird's eye chillies. Cover with the lid and cook for 12–15 minutes on the stove or a shared oven space at 180–200°C fan (400–425°F), basting the fish with the sauce halfway through. The fish should be opaque, cooked through and easy to flake with a fork.

Serve with steamed rice, lots of vegetables and pickles and ferments.

NOTE

If you have a bit more time, "you can slow-cook this for 40 minutes–1 hour over a low heat. The fish will have an amazing melt-in-your-mouth texture and will take on much more of the palm sugar and fish sauce flavour. This can also be made with sliced pork belly and chicken thigh pieces. Let it brown in the pot for 5 minutes first, then stir and cook for 15–20 minutes, adding more coconut water if desired.

Serves 4

BAKED SEA BASS WITH LEEKS, LEMON AND SAMPHIRE

CÁ NƯỚNG CHANH GỪNG

Prep time 15 minutes
Cook time 30 minutes

- 1 tablespoon olive oil
- 1 large or 2 small sea bass (about 1 kg/2 lb 4 oz total), cleaned and gutted
- 30 g (1 oz) fresh ginger root, peeled and sliced
- 1 large leek, trimmed and sliced into 2.5 cm (1 inch) rings
- 1 lemon, zested, then rind roughly removed and sliced into rings
- 100 g (3½ oz) samphire (sea beans)
- 50 g (1¾ oz) spring onions (scallions), sliced lengthways, then soaked in cold water for 5 minutes until they curl
- steamed rice and vegetable side dishes, to serve

FOR THE SAUCE

- 3 tablespoons olive oil
- 2 small round shallots, thinly sliced
- 3 tablespoons light soy sauce
- 2 teaspoons caster (superfine) sugar
- 1 tablespoon black vinegar or cider vinegar
- 1 tablespoon crispy chilli oil (optional)

Steamed fish with ginger and spring onions (scallions) is such a classic Asian favourite. It is usually eaten on special occasions as part of a big feast. I love throwing this baked version together – just bake everything into a roasting tray, then garnish it once baked with curls of spring onion and a scattering of lemon zest for a luscious light feast.

Preheat the oven to 180°C fan (400°F) and use half the oil to grease a baking tray (pan).

Lay the fish on the baking tray and stuff the ginger inside the cavity of the fish. Scatter the leek rings around the fish and place the sliced lemon rings along the body of the fish. Brush over the rest of the olive oil.

Bake the fish in the oven for 25 minutes. In the last 3 minutes, scatter the samphire around the fish.

Once cooked, remove from the oven and transfer to a serving platter (or leave on the baking tray) and dress with the spring onions.

Now, quickly make the sauce. Heat the oil in a small saucepan over a medium heat and cook the shallots for about 5 minutes until golden. Add the soy sauce, sugar, vinegar and crispy chilli oil, if using. Bring to a rolling boil, then pour over the fish, wilting the spring onions. Scatter with the lemon zest.

Serve with rice and lots of vegetable sides.

NOTE

To steam, place a plate inside a bamboo steamer, add the fish and steam for 15–20 minutes, adding the samphire for the last 3 minutes.

Serves 4

Prep time 30–40 minutes
Cook time 20–30 minutes

150 g (5½ oz) red potatoes, peeled and sliced
pinch of sea salt
500 g (1 lb 2 oz) skinless salmon, haddock, cod or coley fillets, cut into chunks
2 small round shallots, sliced
2 garlic cloves, sliced
1 teaspoon mushroom seasoning powder
2 tablespoons premium fish sauce
1½ teaspoons caster (superfine) sugar
1 tablespoon olive oil
1 tablespoon Alsa French baking powder
20 g (¾ oz) dill fronds, sliced into 5 mm (¼ inch) lengths
1 teaspoon freshly ground black pepper
2 bird's eye chillies, sliced diagonally
zest of 1 lime
2 tablespoons vegetable oil, plus extra for frying
Chinese mustard greens, bánh hỏi noodles (page 216) and herbs, to serve

NOTE

The fishcakes can also be steamed for 5 minutes. They can be refrigerated for 3–4 days or frozen and fried at a later date. You can also poach them in broth for noodle soups.

DILL FISHCAKES

CHẢ CÁ THÌ LÀ

Fishcakes are really popular in Vietnam, as are pork patties. The preferred texture is squeaky and chewy rather than soft. This is where the pink French baking powder sachets come into play, as they create the desired clean-cut, dense texture. I prefer my fishcakes to have a looser texture and flakes of fish, hence the potatoes, but feel free to leave out the potato for a more traditional texture. The fishcakes are enjoyed as a filling in summer rolls, mustard green wraps and *bánh mì*, as a topping for noodle soups or dipped in fish sauce and served with steamed rice.

If you have some, you can use leftover mashed potato. Otherwise, put the potatoes in a large saucepan of cold, salted water and bring to the boil, cooking the potatoes for 7 minutes, or until soft. Then drain and coarsely mash them so that there are still some small lumps. Set aside to cool to room temperature.

Put the fish, shallots, garlic, mushroom seasoning, fish sauce, sugar, oil and baking powder into a food processor. Blend until coarsely combined, then transfer the mixture to a bowl. Add the dill, black pepper, chillies, lime zest and the coarsely mashed potatoes. Mix together with a wooden spoon or massage together with your hands. Set aside.

Pour the vegetable oil into a small bowl and grease your hands. Take 2 tablespoons of the mixture and form a patty, ball or sausage-shaped cake. Set aside on a plate, then repeat with the remaining mixture.

Pour 4 cm (1½ inches) oil into a wok and bring up to 160°C (320°F). Fry the fishcakes in batches for about 4 minutes until golden all over, then drain on paper towels. Alternatively, you can pan-fry the fishcakes over a medium heat for 2 minutes on each side until golden.

Serve with mustard green, *bánh hỏi* noodles and herbs.

Serves 4

Prep time 10 minutes
Cook time 20 minutes

2 tablespoons vegetable or extra virgin olive oil
2 sea (gilt-head) bream, cleaned and gutted
1 mango
steamed rice, clear broth, vegetable dishes and pickles, to serve

FOR THE SAUCE

4 garlic cloves, finely chopped
½ mild red chilli or bird's eye chilli, finely chopped
zest and juice of 1 lime
4 tablespoons maple syrup or caster (superfine) sugar
4 tablespoons premium fish sauce
10 g (½ oz) coriander (cilantro) stalks, finely chopped (optional)

PAN-FRIED FISH WITH GREEN MANGO

CÁ CHIÊN NƯỚC MẮM XOÀI

Pan-fried fish is commonly eaten with fish sauce mixed with crushed chillies. It is shared in the middle of the table and we pick the flesh with our chopsticks, dipping it into the sauce before placing it onto our bowls of rice. It is one of those simple and excellent meals, just enjoying the flavours of the fish. Any fish will work for this recipe. If using, green, unripe mango they are typically sour, so the sauce has to be sweeter than usual. Adjust the sweetness according to the sourness of your mango. If you can only get ripe mangoes, then decrease the quantity of maple syrup.

Pour the vegetable oil into a large frying pan over a medium heat.

Pat the fish dry with paper towels, then add to the pan. Shallow-fry for 7–10 minutes on each side, or until the skin is golden and crispy.

Meanwhile, peel the mango and cut them into thin slices. Arrange the slices on a large platter, leaving the centre empty for the fish.

Prepare the sauce by mixing together all the ingredients, except the lime zest, in a bowl. Taste and adjust to perfect the balance of sweet and sour flavours. Some limes may have more or less juice than others.

Sprinkle the lime zest over the mango slices.

When the fish is cooked, place it onto the platter and pour over the sauce. Serve immediately with steamed rice, a clear broth and plenty of steamed, fried or poached vegetables and pickles.

NOTE

Feel free to use fillets of sea bream, sea bass, trout or tilapia. Simply fry for 3 minutes on each side.

Instead of mango, a bed of watercress or rocket (arugula) is also delicious.

STEAMED EGG TERRINE

CHẢ TRỨNG

Serves 4

Prep time 15 minutes
Cook time 40 minutes

- 1 teaspoon vegetable oil
- 1 tablespoon olive oil
- 2 small round shallots, thinly sliced
- 4 garlic cloves, finely chopped
- 4 large eggs
- 1½ tablespoon premium fish sauce
- 1 tablespoon caster (superfine) sugar
- 1 teaspoon sea salt, plus extra for the egg yolks
- 1 teaspoon freshly ground black pepper
- ¼ teaspoon mushroom seasoning powder (optional)
- 25 g (1 oz) dried wood ear mushrooms (black fungus), soaked for 30 minutes in warm water, then finely chopped
- 25 g (1 oz) glass noodles, soaked for 10 minutes in warm water, then cut into 1 cm (½ inch) pieces
- 1 tablespoon cornflour (cornstarch)
- 200 g (7 oz) minced (ground) pork or chicken
- 2 egg yolks
- broken rice, vegetables, ferments and pickles, to serve

This modest and frugal dish can be simply enjoyed with steamed rice and makes a delicious midweek dinner with mostly pantry ingredients. Swap out the minced (ground) pork for chicken or increase your plant intake by replacing it with chopped mushrooms and greens. My mum used to make smaller portions steamed in rice bowls if she intended to serve this with lots of other dishes in a family-style sharing table. Enjoy with plenty of ferments or pickles and an array of uncooked and cooked vegetables. Any leftovers can be used in *bánh mì* and summer rolls or as a topping for noodle soups or fried noodles.

Grease a deep, heatproof bowl (or loaf tin/pan or pie dish) with the vegetable oil and set aside.

Heat the olive oil in a frying pan over a medium heat and brown the shallots for 5 minutes, then add the garlic and cook for a further 2 minutes. Remove from the heat and set aside.

In a large bowl, mix together the eggs, fish sauce, sugar, salt, black pepper and mushroom seasoning powder, if using. Add the shallots and garlic, wood ear mushrooms, glass noodles and cornflour and stir well.

Add the minced meat and stir well to combine. Pour the mixture into the prepared bowl.

Prepare a steamer and place the bowl inside. Steam for 25–30 minutes until set, making sure the water in the steamer does not evaporate. When it's ready, the juices will run clear when you insert a skewer into the centre.

Meanwhile, beat the egg yolks with a pinch of salt.

Pour the egg yolks over the terrine and steam for a further 5 minutes.

Serve with broken rice, vegetables of any manner, ferments and pickles.

NOTES

This can also be cooked in the oven in a loaf tin (pan). Preheat the oven to 200°C fan (425°F). Place the tin in a bain-marie, cover with foil and bake for 40–45 minutes. Pour over the egg yolks and return to the oven to cook, uncovered, for a further 7–10 minutes with the door ajar.

For a vegetarian alternative, swap the meat for a variety of mushrooms fried with vegetarian oyster sauce or add fried and chopped tofu or frozen diced vegetables.

6 WEEKEND FEASTS

WEEKEND FEASTS

My love for entertaining stems from the family-style feasts I have shared with friends and family throughout my life. The joy of eating together took grip of me from a young age. When I was younger, I had to go with my mum to all her dinner parties in Hackney council flats. She and her friends would order in roast duck and crispy pork belly from Chinese takeaways (takeouts) and someone would visit the Chinese supermarket to buy crabs, tiger prawns (shrimp), mussels and so on. The floor would be covered in baskets of home-grown herbs, washed and clustered together. They would sing their hearts out on the karaoke machine to sad, funny and cheering songs and they would dance around the feast, coming back to pick at the food all night long, finishing it all off with a warm noodle soup later in the evening.

As I got older, I have always craved the candle-lit dinner parties I used to see through the windows of beautiful Victorian or Georgian homes on the cold winter commutes. The kitchens were often in the basement and if I walked slowly enough while passing their large sash windows, among the bushes of rosemary and snowdrops, I could peer right through to the dining rooms where people would clink their red wine glasses and serve each other a carving of meat and a spoonful of peas.

When I visited Vietnam, my cousin Thuý often arranged a welcome of coconut water, mango and rambutans. She would gather huge feasts on a rug of newspaper, ordering roasted meats, pickles, all the best seafood and made hotpots, laying out herbs, lettuce wraps, toppings and rice paper for everyone to make their own rolls. We would sit around on the floor, crossed legged and slouching, clinking beer glasses dripping with condensation, giggling.

In my first flat in London Fields, my friends and I celebrated together, at the peak of our youth, enjoying crunchy flavoursome salads, crispy belly of pork and baked sea bass. We sang, danced on tables, and those who played musical instruments jammed out to their hearts' content on the upright piano my mother had saved up for all those years ago, hoping that I would be talented. We dragged out pots and pans for the drummer and borrowed the neighbour's guitars. 'This is the best night of my life!' someone said, and I wholeheartedly agreed.

In my small kitchen, I unearthed my appetite for cooking. I pulled myself from the soils of love and heartache, ended my boutique business and decided to do what I loved. I started my supper club, filling my home with strangers to host dinner parties like the ones I had seen through the windows all those years before. Everything poured out – the food I was feeding was me. The kitchen was a place I could truly myself.

Serves as many as you like

BÁNH HỎI PLATTER AND SUMMER ROLL PARTY

TIỆC BÁNH HỎI VÀ GỎI CUỐN

Prep time	up to you
Cook time	up to you

sheets of bánh hỏi noodles (about 6–10 per person)
variety of herbs
salad leaves
sheets of rice paper

FOR THE SPRING ONION OIL (PAGE 208)

FOR THE POACHED PORK BELLY (OPTIONAL)

pork belly
sea salt
fresh ginger root, sliced (a thumb-sized per 1 kg/2 lb 4 oz of meat)

FOR THE POACHED PRAWNS (OPTIONAL)

coconut water or water, for cooking
raw shell-on prawns (shrimp), trimmed

FOR THE FRIED TOFU (OPTIONAL)

medium-firm tofu
generous amount of olive oil
pinch of salt

FOR THE NƯỚC MẮM

2 bird's eye chillies, finely chopped
2 garlic cloves, crushed
3 tablespoons caster (superfine) sugar
3 tablespoons lime juice
4 tablespoons premium fish sauce
2 tablespoons toasted sesame seeds
a few coriander (cilantro) stalks, thinly sliced
2 tablespoons hot water

FOR THE VINAIGRETTE

2 small round shallots, finely diced
10 g (½ oz) cucumber, finely diced
30 g (1 oz) carrot, thinly crinkle cut or cut into circles or cubes
1 tablespoon caster (superfine) sugar
3 tablespoons cider vinegar
1 tablespoon premium fish sauce
3 tablespoon hot water

Bánh hỏi are sheets of quick-cooking rice vermicelli noodles that have been woven together and then cut into little sheets.

Choose a couple of feast option recipes to make, such as Char Sui Crispy Pork Belly (page 154), Battered Spring Onions (page 42) and Salmon and Avocado Summer Rolls (page 56). They are fabulous on platters spread across the table with noodles, vegetables and rice paper for making wraps and summer rolls. I haven't included quantities for most of the elements as this is a feast, so it's up to you on how much you want to make. The nước mắm and vinaigrette both serve 4. Enjoy the assembly.

To prepare the noodles, see page 146 for instructions.

Next, make the spring onion oil. See page 208 for instructions.

Either roll up the noodles or place them flat on platters and smother them with the spring onion oil.

To poach the pork belly, if using, bring a large saucepan of water to the boil and add the pork, salt and ginger. Cover and simmer for 15 minutes, then remove from the heat and let the residual heat cook the pork for a further 15–20 minutes. Once cooked, place into a bowl of iced water for 15 minutes before slicing into thin, bite-sized pieces.

To cook the king prawns, if using, bring a saucepan of coconut water or water to the boil, then add the prawns. Swirl the water, then cover and cook for 2–3 minutes until the prawns are pink and opaque. Drain and set aside to cool to room temperature.

To fry the tofu, if using, heat a generous amount of olive oil and a pinch of salt in a large wok or frying pan over a medium heat, then fry the tofu for about 8 minutes on each side until golden. Transfer to paper towels to drain.

To make the sauces, mix together the ingredients in small bowls.

Serve the noodles, salad leaves and herbs, rice paper, meats, optional feast dishes and anything else you fancy in the middle of the table for everyone to help themselves to.

Serves 2

BIRTHDAY STEAK AND EGGS BRUNCH

BÒ NÉ

Prep time 15 minutes
Cook time 10 minutes

- 2 x 100 g (3½ oz) bavette (flank) steaks (or another cut if preferred), at room temperature
- 3 tablespoons olive oil
- 1 onion, sliced lengthways into 8 pieces
- 2 garlic cloves, grated
- 1 teaspoon freshly ground black pepper, plus extra as needed
- 1 tablespoon Maggi liquid seasoning, plus extra as needed
- 2–4 eggs (any size)
- 2 seasonal tomatoes, sliced
- pinch of sea salt
- 1 tablespoon kimchi or sauerkraut (shop-bought or homemade, page 207; optional)
- 2 quick-pickled beetroot (beets) or carrots (optional)
- 2 slices of Comté
- 2 Laughing Cow cheese triangles (optional)
- salted butter, to serve
- 2 Vietnamese baguettes or crusty rolls, to serve

NOTE

For a vegetarian alternative, use king oyster mushrooms, sliced lengthways, instead of steak. Or simply enjoy sunny side up eggs and great tomatoes on any occasion.

Steak, chips (French fries) and eggs is a common treat in Vietnam; just one of the many French culinary influences. It's usually enjoyed with iced coffee and a good hang out with friends or loved ones on a special occasion or weekends.

Heat a frying pan over a high heat. Put the steaks onto a plate and brush with 2 tablespoons of the oil, then add to the pan along with the onion and any oil left on the plate. Sprinkle over half the garlic, black pepper and Maggi seasoning. After 2 minutes, flip the steak and repeat. Remove the steak and onions from the pan and set aside to rest.

Add the remaining oil to the pan and fry the eggs, sunny side up.

Divide the tomatoes between plates and season with the salt, then add the kimchi or sauerkraut and pickles, if using, and the cheeses. Have the butter, extra black pepper and a bottle of Maggi at hand.

Slice the steak against the grain and place on the plates. Serve with the baguettes or rolls.

Serves 4

SHAKING LEMONGRASS BEEF WITH BETEL LEAVES

Prep time 15 minutes, plus 1 hour marinating time
Cook time 10–15 minutes

600 g (1 lb 5 oz) fillet or rib eye steak, cut into 2 cm (¾ inch) cubes
1 tablespoon oyster sauce
2 tablespoons Maggi liquid seasoning or light soy sauce
4 garlic cloves, crushed
1 round shallot, finely chopped
30 g (1 oz) lemongrass, finely chopped
½ teaspoon caster (superfine) sugar
2 teaspoons sesame oil
1 heaped teaspoon freshly ground black pepper
2 tablespoons vegetable oil
4 spring onions (scallions), cut into 4 cm (1½ inch) lengths
100 g (3½ oz) betel leaves
rice, salad or rice vermicelli salad, to serve

This recipe combines the famous shaking beef with its cousin *bò lá lốt* (beef wrapped in betel leaves). A tremendously fragrant ingredient when cooked, the aroma of betel leaves reminds me of the smells of the Vietnamese countryside and homes filled with incense and burning cinnamon. This is quicker and easier as the flavour of the leaves will be present without the job of rolling.

Put the beef into a bowl and add the oyster sauce, Maggi liquid seasoning or soy sauce, garlic, shallot, lemongrass, sugar, sesame oil and black pepper. Stir well, then cover and set aside to marinate for at least 1 hour at room temperature. If you want to leave it longer, put it into the refrigerator, then bring it to room temperature before cooking.

You will need to cook the beef in batches, depending on the size of your pan. Heat a frying pan over a high heat for a few minutes until very hot. Add 1 tablespoon of the vegetable oil, then add some of the spring onions and a batch of beef cubes, making sure they are not too crowded together. Leave to sear for 30 seconds, then add some of the betel leaves and stir-fry for 1 minute. Continue to cook for a further 1½ minutes, shaking the pan vigorously for 10 seconds every 30 seconds, until the beef is medium-rare. Set aside on a plate, then repeat with the remaining ingredients. When all the beef is cooked, pour any juices left in the pan over the plate.

Serve immediately with rice, salad or rice vermicelli salad.

Serves 4

Prep time 15 minutes
Cook time 55 minutes

80 g (2¾ oz) lemon curd
2 tablespoons premium fish sauce
30 g (1 oz) lemongrass, finely chopped
1.5 kg (3 lb 5 oz) pork ribs, untrimmed
1 garlic bulb, halved
8 small round shallots, peeled and halved
1 lemon, zested and then sliced into rings
1½ teaspoons sea salt
1 teaspoon freshly ground black pepper
20 g (¾ oz) salted or unsalted butter
1 spring onion (scallion), sliced diagonally
1 red chilli, sliced diagonally (optional)
steamed or blanched vegetables, to serve

LEMON CURD ROAST PORK RIBS WITH GARLIC BUTTER

SƯỜN NƯỚNG CHANH BƠ TỎI

The sweet and sour combination of this roast is an absolute winner. It is really easy to prepare and absolutely guaranteed to please your guests or enjoy midweek with rice. You can also use one large chicken instead of ribs if you prefer. I love serving this with garlic and rosemary roast potatoes or lemon and thyme chips (fries).

Preheat the oven to 200°C fan (425°F).

Mix together the lemon curd, fish sauce and lemongrass in a small bowl, then set aside.

Put the ribs into a large roasting tin and smother them with the lemon curd mixture on both sides. Save 4 garlic cloves and place the rest of the halved bulb underneath the ribs. Scatter around the shallots and lemon rings. Sprinkle with the salt and pepper. Roast for 45–50 minutes, basting after 30 minutes at least twice.

Once cooked, remove the ribs from the oven and set aside to rest for at least 10 minutes before carving.

Finely chop the reserved garlic cloves. Heat the butter in a small frying pan over a low heat and fry the garlic for 1 minute until golden, then add the spring onion and cook until wilted. Brush the garlic butter all over the ribs and baste them their lemony juices.

Sprinkle over the chilli (if using) and lemon zest, then serve with vegetables.

Serves 4–6

CHAR SIU CRISPY PORK BELLY

THỊT QUAY XÁ XÍU

Prep time 15 minutes, plus 2½ hours marinating and resting time
Cook time 1 hour 20 minutes

- 1 kg (2 lb 4 oz) pork belly, scored
- 100 g (3½ oz) roast red pork seasoning mix (see below if you can't find this)
- 4 tablespoons light soy sauce
- 1 tablespoon water
- 1 tablespoon cider or white wine vinegar
- 2 tablespoons sea salt

I love Chinese char siu pork, but I love the fatty, crispy belly even more, so this combines the two. It's a winner at every dinner party or the perfect weekend dinner treat. Serve with Vermicelli Noodle Salad Bowls (page 210) or steamed rice and vegetables or with *bánh hỏi* (page 216).

Bring a large saucepan of water to the boil, add the pork and simmer for 10 minutes, then remove from the water. Rinse under cold water, then pat dry with paper towels. Stab and roughly score the meat side.

Combine the roast red pork seasoning mix, soy sauce and water in a small bowl, then spread the mixture evenly onto the surface of a tray (pan) or box that fits the meat. Put the pork belly on top, skin side up, and brush the marinade onto the sides of the meat. The seasoning mixture should cover the flesh side and leave the skin dry.

Rub the vinegar all over the skin and sprinkle with 1 tablespoon of the salt. Marinate at room temperature, uncovered, for at least 2 hours, or overnight in the refrigerator, covered, dabbing off any moisture from the skin every 30 minutes when you're able and rubbing on the remaining salt.

When you're ready to cook, preheat the oven to 220°C fan (475°F). Transfer the pork to a roasting tin lined with baking parchment. Pat the skin dry with paper towels, then roast in the oven for 1 hour 10 minutes. Remove from the oven and set aside to rest for at least 30 minutes. Slice when at room temperature.

NOTE

If you can't get hold of the roast red pork seasoning mix, use 1 teaspoon Chinese five spice, 2 tablespoons garlic powder, 2 tablespoons brown sugar, 2 tablespoons dark soy sauce, 2 tablespoons tomato ketchup and ¼ teaspoon red food colouring.

Serves 4

ROAST PLUM AND CLEMENTINE DUCK WITH NEW POTATOES

VỊT NƯỚNG KHOAI TÂY

Prep time 15 minutes
Cook time 1 hour

FOR THE DUCK

- 4 duck legs (about 900 g/ 2 lb total), at room temperature
- 2 clementines, zested and sliced (with peel) into 1 cm (½ inch) rings
- 2 garlic bulbs, halved

FOR THE SAUCE

- 2 tablespoons olive oil
- 180 ml (6 fl oz/¾ cup) plum sauce
- 30 g (1 oz) fresh ginger root, peeled and grated
- 4 tablespoons oyster sauce
- zest and juice of 2 clementines
- sea salt and freshly ground black pepper

FOR THE POTATOES

- 3 tablespoons olive oil
- 1 kg (2 lb 4 oz) new potatoes (I use Jersey Royals), halved
- 1 tablespoon sea salt
- 1 red onion, sliced
- 2 spring onions (scallions), sliced
- knob of salted butter (optional)

FOR THE CABBAGE

- 350 g (12 oz) red cabbage, thinly sliced
- 2 teaspoons olive oil
- 2 shallots, sliced
- 2 tablespoons light soy sauce
- 1 tablespoon cider vinegar
- 2 tablespoons kimchi (shop-bought or homemade, page 207; optional)

TO SERVE

- steamed vegetables, such as Tenderstem broccoli (broccolini), carrots, sweetheart (pointed/ hispi) cabbage, fine green beans

I love to marry Vietnamese flavours with traditional English dishes like a Sunday roast, in the same way that the Vietnamese combined their cuisine with that of the French for a century. This warming and comforting meal brings much contentment to chilly evenings and special occasions.

Preheat the oven to 200°C fan (425°F).

Put the duck legs into a roasting tin with the clementines and garlic. Mix together all the ingredients for the sauce, except the clementine zest, and smother the duck legs with it on both sides. Roast in the oven for 50 minutes, then remove and allow to rest for 10–15 minutes.

While the duck is cooking, pour the oil for the potatoes into a separate roasting tin and add to the oven to heat up.

Put the potatoes into a saucepan of cold water with the salt and bring to a simmer, then cover and cook for 25 minutes. Drain the potatoes, let it steam off for 5 minutes then carefully add to the hot oil. Use a spoon to toss the potatoes in the oil, then scatter over the red onion and roast in the oven for 25 minutes.

Meanwhile, bring a large saucepan of water to the boil and simmer the red cabbage for 10 minutes, then drain. Add the oil to the same pan and fry the shallots for 5 minutes until golden, then add the soy sauce and vinegar and add the cabbage back in. Mix well, then stir in the kimchi, if using.

To serve, scatter the spring onions over the potatoes and add the butter, if using, letting it melt over the potatoes. Sprinkle the clementine zest over the duck legs and serve both with the cabbage and steamed vegetables.

Serves 4

LEMONGRASS AND STAR ANISE CHICKEN STEW OR PIE

GÀ HẦM SẢ VÀ HOA HỒI

This is a lovely fresh and light stew that can also be turned into a comforting and soothing pie for colder evenings. It is quick and easy to prepare ahead of time, then all you have to do is let it cook. This is one of the recipes that can be cooked in the oven with other things to help you get ahead of the game. If serving as a stew, I love this with flat rice noodles, rice or buttered baguette. If you add the pie top, enjoy with lots of steamed vegetables and homemade chips (French Fries) (page 164) or mashed potatoes.

Prep time 30 minutes
Cook time 40 minutes – 1 hour 5 minutes

- 2 tablespoons extra virgin olive oil
- 800 g (1 lb 12 oz) boneless chicken thighs, cut into 5 cm (2 inch) chunks, skin on or off
- 4 small round shallots, sliced
- 30 g (1 oz) lemongrass, finely chopped
- 4 garlic cloves, sliced
- 1 teaspoon celery salt or sea salt
- 1½ teaspoons ground cumin
- 1½ teaspoons sweet paprika
- 300 g (10½ oz) new potatoes, cut into bite-sized cubes
- 300 g (10½ oz) carrots, cut into 2 cm (¾ inch) rounds
- 1 tablespoon cornflour (cornstarch)
- 400 ml (14 fl oz/generous 1½ cups) coconut water or chicken stock
- 1 chicken stock cube, crumbled
- 3 star anise
- 3 tablespoons premium fish sauce
- 60 g (2 oz) cavolo nero (lacinato kale) or kale, sliced
- juice of ½ lime

FOR THE PIE TOPPING

- 1 x 320 g (11¼ oz) packet of puff pastry
- 1 egg yolk, beaten

Heat the oil in a casserole dish (Dutch oven) over a medium-high heat and brown the chicken thighs on all sides for 8–10 minutes. Add the shallots and lemongrass and fry for 5 minutes until they start to turn golden, then add the garlic, salt, cumin, sweet paprika, new potatoes and carrots. Give this a good stir so that everything is coated evenly.

Mix the cornflour with a little of the coconut water or stock until it has dissolved, then pour it and the rest of the coconut water or stock into the pan. Crumble in the chicken stock cube and stir well. Add the star anise, cover tightly and simmer over a low heat for 20 minutes.

After this time, season the stew with the fish sauce and throw in the cavolo nero or kale. Give it a good stir, then cook for a further 5 minutes. Remove from the heat and allow the residual heat to finish cooking the greens.

If you wish to make a pie, transfer the mixture to a pie dish and cover with the puff pastry. Decorate the surface with the back of a knife, if you would like, and brush over the egg yolk. Bake in a 180°C fan (400°F) oven for 25 minutes.

To serve, squeeze over the lime juice.

NOTE

Feel free to jazz it up by adding Thai basil or coriander (cilantro). You can also add a good helping of frozen peas to the mix for extra greens.

Serves 4

PRAWN, SWEET POTATO AND COURGETTE FRITTERS

BÁNH TÔM

Prep time 20 minutes
Cook time 20 minutes

300 g (10½ oz/scant 1¼ cups) rice flour
2 tablespoons cornflour (cornstarch)
¼ teaspoon ground turmeric
2 teaspoons sea salt
½ teaspoon freshly ground black pepper
300 ml (10 fl oz/1¼ cups) cold sparkling water
vegetable oil, for frying
160 g (5½ oz) sweet potatoes, cut into 5 mm (¼ inch) thick batons
160 g (5½ oz) purple sweet potatoes or parsnips, cut into 5 mm (¼ inch) thick batons
8 spring onions (scallions), sliced lengthways
160 g (5½ oz) courgettes (zucchini), cut into 5 mm (¼ inch) thick batons
300 g (10½ oz) raw shell-on prawns (shrimp), trimmed
Vermicelli Noodle Salad Bowls (page 210) or an array of beautiful leaves, herbs, pickles and kimchi (shop-bought or homemade, page 207), to serve

FOR THE DIPPING SAUCE

1 bird's eye chilli, finely chopped
1 garlic clove, crushed
2 tablespoons maple syrup (or anything sweet and syrupy)
2 tablespoons premium fish sauce
finely chopped zest and juice of ½ lime or lemon
sprig of mint leaves, thinly sliced
a few coriander (cilantro) stalks, thinly sliced

These should be enjoyed the Vietnamese way, by slowly peeling the prawns (shrimp) and sucking on their juices and then devouring the flesh and vegetables with a tons of herbs. Feel free to use shell-off prawns.

First, make the dipping sauce by combing all the ingredients in a jar and shaking together.

Combine the rice flour, cornflour, turmeric, salt and black pepper in a bowl and stir together with a whisk. Slowly pour in the sparkling water, whisking constantly, until you have a smooth, thick batter.

Pour 2.5 cm (1 inch) oil into a wok and bring up to 180°C (350°F).

Put two or three pieces of sweet potato, spring onion, courgette and a prawn into the bowl of batter and coat all the pieces. Gather onto a large spoon, sliding away any excess batter, and gently lower into the oil. Fry for 3–4 minutes on each side until golden, then remove with a spider or slotted spoon and place on paper towels to drain. Repeat with the remaining vegetables and prawns.

Serve warm or at room temperature with the noodle salad or with leaves, herbs and pickles.

Makes 12 spring rolls (serves 4)

HADDOCK SPRING ROLLS

CHẢ GIÒ CÁ

Prep time 25 minutes
Cook time 20 minutes

400 g (14 oz) skinless haddock fillet, cut into 1 x 5 cm (½ x 2 inch) strips
½ teaspoon ground white pepper
½ teaspoon celery salt
pinch of sea salt
2 spring onions (scallions), sliced
12 x 22 cm (8½ inch) sheets of rice paper
½ carrot, julienned
80 g (2¾ oz) sugar snap peas, sliced
20 g (¾ oz) Vietnamese coriander (cilantro) leaves
vegetable oil, for frying

FOR THE DIPPING SAUCE

1 tablespoon clear honey
zest of 1 lime or lemon juice, plus 1 tablespoon juice
1 tablespoon premium fish sauce
3 tablespoons coconut water
1 teaspoon sesame seeds
½ bird's eye chilli, thinly sliced on the diagonal

These are our household favourite with a vermicelli noodle salad for a tasty Friday-night fish dinner – a bit like fish and chips, but the Vietnamese way. The textures are amazing, with the crispiness on the outside contrasting with the soft fish and crunchy vegetables inside. Perfect served in a cool salad bowl with plenty of fresh herbs and vegetables or with salad and herb wraps.

Put the haddock, white pepper, celery salt, salt and spring onions into a bowl and stir together.

Quickly dip a sheet of rice paper into water to moisten it, then transfer to a board or large plate. Just below the middle of the paper, place two pieces of haddock, a thin layer of carrot and sugar snap peas and a couple of Vietnamese coriander leaves.

Fold the sides in, then fold over the bottom and roll up as tightly as you can. Repeat with the remaining rice paper and fillings.

Pour 4 cm (1½ inches) oil into a wok and bring up to 180°C (350°F).

Gently place three or four rolls into the pan, being careful not to let them stick together or crowd the pan. Fry for 3 minutes until crisp and puffy, using a pair of cooking chopsticks or tongs to turn the rolls so that they cook evenly on all sides. Remove with a spider or slotted spoon and place on paper towels to drain.

Mix all the ingredients for the dipping sauce together and serve in individual dipping bowls with the spring rolls.

NOTE

Cod, salmon, hake, lemon sole or prawns all work well in this recipe too. For a vegetarian alternative, use tofu or roasted cauliflower.

MARINADED SASHIMI AND CHIPS

CÁ SỐNG VÀ KHOAI TÂY CHIÊN

Serves 4
(or 2 greedy people because it's so good)

Prep time 25 minutes
Cook time 1 hour

FOR THE CHIPS

3 tablespoons olive oil
1 kg (2 lb 4 oz) red potatoes, peeled and cut into fat chips
1 tablespoon sea salt, plus extra as needed
knob of salted butter
1 tablespoon onion vinegar (optional)

FOR THE WASABI MAYO

4 tablespoons mayonnaise
2 teaspoons wasabi paste

FOR THE FISH

30 g (1 oz) fresh ginger root, peeled and grated
2 teaspoons wasabi paste
2 tablespoons Japanese nama (unpasteurised) soy sauce
150 ml (5½ fl oz/scant ⅔ cup) orange juice
400 g (14 oz) sashimi-grade tuna or salmon, cut into 1 cm (½ inch) cubes
2 spring onions (scallions), thinly sliced

I created this recipe after eating one of the most memorable meals I've ever had at a friend's house. Kaoru loves to cook and she made an exquisite Japanese feast. I asked what ingredients she had used and she told me there was soy sauce, a bit of mirin... a long pause followed before a different conversation started. Through experimentation, I came to this, and it is so gorgeous with homemade chips (fries). If you can't be bothered to make chips, get some from the chippy and drench them in onion vinegar, then reheat them in the oven when you get home. That extra bit of vinegar brings utter perfection to this dish. It's a real treat!

Preheat the oven to 200°C fan (425°F). Pour the olive oil into a large roasting tin and place in the oven.

Rinse the potatoes to wash off any starch, then add to a saucepan of boiling water along with the salt. Simmer for 7–8 minutes until just fork-tender. Drain, let it steam off for 5 minutes and return to the pan with the butter. Shake the pan to fluff up the potatoes, then carefully transfer them to the tin of hot oil – it should sizzle. Bake in the oven for about 45 minutes until golden and crisp.

Meanwhile, make the wasabi mayo by mixing together the mayonnaise and wasabi in a small bowl.

For the fish, mix together the ginger, wasabi, soy sauce and orange juice in a bowl. Add the fish and fold into the sauce.

Sprinkle the spring onions over the fish, then serve with the hot chips, a generous squirt of onion vinegar (if using) and a sprinkling of sea salt.

NOTE

Mix the sauce and the fish together just before serving. If you need to do so ahead of time, make sure it is no more than 30 minutes before you will eat.

Serves 4

SWEET AND SOUR SEAFOOD HOTPOT

LẨU HẢI SẢN CHUA NGỌT

Prep time 30 minutes–1 hour
Cook time 15 minutes, plus communal cook time

This is a great celebration feast – it's the ultimate family-style sharing meal and there is much enjoyment to be found in cooking at the table and then slowly peeling the seafood as you sit around the table eating together. You can do as much or as little as you like here. Fill the table with a huge variety of ingredients as well as plenty of herbs, a variety of mushrooms, tofu, noodles and condiments, such as chilli oil and lime, or simply use a handful of things that you have or is in season.

- 6 small round shallots, sliced
- ½ garlic bulb, cloves peeled
- 20 g (¾ oz) fresh ginger root, peeled and sliced
- 2 tablespoons olive oil
- 4 tomatoes, cut into wedges
- 1 x 230 g (8¼ oz) tin of pineapple chunks in juice
- 1.5 litres (50 fl oz/6¼ cups) chicken, pork, fish or vegetable stock
- 30 g (1 oz) lemongrass, stalks bashed
- 20 g (¾ oz) rock sugar
- 2 tablespoons premium fish sauce

FOR THE SAUCE

- 4 garlic cloves, finely chopped
- 4 bird's eye chillies, finely chopped
- zest and juice of 1 lime
- 4 tablespoons maple syrup or clear honey
- 4 tablespoons premium fish sauce
- 10 g (½ oz) coriander stalks, finely sliced (optional)

TO SERVE

- a variety of raw seafood, such as shell-on king prawns (shrimp), langoustines, scallops, squid rings, razor clams, mussels and clams
- a variety of vegetables such as Chinese mustard greens, morning glory, pak choi and Tenderstem broccoli (broccolini)
- a variety of herbs, such as Thai basil, mint, coriander (cilantro),
- a variety of mushrooms, such as king oyster and shiitake
- fried tofu chunks or shop-bought tofu puffs
- noodles or rice
- a variety of condiments

Place the shallots, garlic and ginger into a food processor and blend to a smooth paste.

Heat the olive oil in a large saucepan or stockpot over a medium heat and fry the paste for 5 minutes until fragrant and golden, then add the tomatoes and pineapple chunks along with their juice. Fry for a couple of minutes, then add the stock. Throw in the bashed lemongrass and rock sugar and bring to a simmer for 10 minutes. Season with the fish sauce.

Assemble all the seafood elements on a large platter. Place the vegetables, herbs, mushrooms, tofu and noodles or rice on separate platters.

Make the sauce by mixing together all the ingredients in a bowl, then serve in individual dipping bowls. Arrange any other condiments.

Place a tabletop hob (hotplate) in the middle of the table and set the pan of hot broth on top. Bring the broth to the boil, then allow everyone to pick and cook their ingredients.

7 DESSERTS & DRINKS

DESSERTS & DRINKS

'What's for dessert?' Olive would enquire, mouth full of dinner, hands gripping onto a branch of drooping broccoli. Desserts are equally as important as the dinner itself. My daughter Olive eats well balanced meals – she loves her vegetables and loves desserts with equal measure. Something sweet brings a certain joy to her, to round off the evening and whatever the day was, a satisfaction before bedtime.

Olive loves coconut rice pudding, be it with sweetcorn or purple sweet potatoes, tapioca puddings and devours avocado shakes. She jumps with joy over cake, especially anything infused with pandan, and dreams of the occasion we can make bubble tea together (page 190). On Sunday mornings, while she dances and plays, I make a batch of Pandan Mochi Waffles (page 172), which she happily enjoys for breakfasts throughout the week, lightly toasted and served with sliced fruit, berries and a drizzle of honey. On my free days, she loves to receive a squidgy Pandan Mochi ball (page 175), covered with desiccated (dried shredded) coconut or a small square of homemade Vietnamese Coffee Tiramisu (page 178), which we share and have teaspoon thumb wars over. She divides a portion of what she can have and an allotment of what I can share. She counts the mouthfuls I am allowed for it is all too delicious to lose. Sharing makes us sit closely together, indulging in moments of pleasure. Cakes never taste as good when the whole lot is yours, she says.

The thing is, I stop for the day when we relish our desserts together; it is our pleasure time, a contentment, and it seems to complete her, just like it did me when my mother delivered a bowl of Tofu Pudding with Ginger Syrup (page 181) after one of her gorgeous dinners. It was and is an I-Love-You, everything-is-OK dessert.

PANDAN MOCHI WAFFLES

BÁNH KẸP LÁ DỨA

Makes 4–5

Prep time 10 minutes
Cook time 30 minutes

150 g (5½ oz/1 cup minus 2 heaped tablespoons) glutinous rice flour
50 g (1¾ oz/scant ½ cup) self-raising flour
1 teaspoon baking powder
2 tablespoons cornflour (cornstarch) or potato starch
2 large eggs
60 g (2 oz/⅓ cup) brown sugar (or to taste)
300 ml (10 fl oz/1¼ cups) coconut milk
50 ml (1¾ fl oz/3½ tablespoons) Pandan Extract (page 209, or use ½ teaspoon shop-bought)

TO SERVE (OPTIONAL)

fresh fruit or berries
maple syrup or honey

Waffles are a popular sweet snack that are sold everywhere on the streets of Vietnam. Their waffly smell is what draws a crowd. Sometimes they are banana or vanilla flavour, but my favourite is, of course, pandan. These mochi waffles are soft and chewy on the inside and crispy on the outside. I make a batch of these and have them for dessert over a few days, lightly toasted and served with a fruit salad, homemade yoghurt and a helping of honey or maple syrup.

Preheat a waffle maker to medium-high.

Combine the glutinous rice flour with the self-raising flour, baking powder and cornflour or potato starch.

In a separate bowl, whisk together the eggs with the sugar for about 5 minutes until pale and fluffy, then add the coconut milk and pandan extract. Whisk to combine for a minute, then add to the dry ingredients, whisking until lump-free. It should be slightly stiff like the consistency of just-whipped cream or wall paint.

Add 4–6 tablespoons of the mixture to the waffle maker and cook for 5–6 minutes until light brown.

Serve warm or at room temperature with fruit or berries and maple syrup or honey, if you would like.

NOTE

This works well without eggs for a vegan version.

Makes about 20 balls

PANDAN MOCHI BALLS WITH PALM SUGAR AND PEANUT BUTTER

MOCHI NHÂN ĐẬU PHỘNG

Prep time 30–40 minutes
Cook time 10 minutes

- 300 g (10½ oz/scant 1¾ cups) glutinous rice flour, plus extra for dusting
- 140 g (5 oz/scant ⅔ cup) caster (superfine) sugar
- 100 ml (3½ fl oz/scant ½ cup) coconut milk (or 170 ml/6 fl oz/ ¾ cup if using shop-bought pandan extract)
- ¼ teaspoon shop-bought pandan extract, or homemade 70 ml (2½ fl oz) Pandan Extract (page 209)
- 50 g (1¾ oz) smooth or crunchy peanut butter
- 40 g (1½ oz) palm sugar, cut into 1 cm (½ inch) pieces
- 100 g (3½ oz/scant 1¼ cups) desiccated (dried shredded) coconut

This is an excellent play on textures: grainy desiccated (dried shredded) coconut contrasts with the smooth, sweet dough, which is filled with hot, melting peanut butter and crunchy palm sugar. The irresistible perfume of pandan will fill your house with joy.

Combine the glutinous rice flour and sugar in a large bowl.

Pour the coconut milk into a small saucepan over a medium-low heat and bring to a simmer, then add the pandan extract and pour the mixture into the flour and sugar. Mix well, then knead for 5 minutes until it is smooth and looks like sugar fondant but feels like the softest dough.

Divide the dough into three pieces and roll each one into a 2.5 cm (1 inch) thick sausage. Using a knife or dough scraper, divide the sausages into 2 cm (¾ inch) pieces.

Take one piece and roll it into a ball, then flatten it. Add ½ teaspoon of peanut butter and a piece of palm sugar. Pinch the dough together to cover the filling, then roll it into a ball using both your palms. Place into an airtight container and repeat with the remaining dough pieces.

Spread out the desiccated coconut on a plate.

When ready to cook, bring a large saucepan of water to the boil and gently drop in some of the mochi balls. Make sure you don't overcrowd the pan. Cook for a minute, then use a spoon to gently move them around as they may stick to the bottom. Cook for a further 4–5 minutes until they float to the top, then cook for a further minute before fishing them out with a slotted spoon onto the plate of desiccated coconut. Leave to cool for 5 minutes, then roll them in the coconut.

Serve warm or at room temperature.

NOTE

Different brands of glutinous rice flour vary. Some will leave the dough stiff, firm and dense and will require more moisture (if this is the case, add a little boiling water). The final dough should be soft and cloud-like.

Serves 4

Prep time 5 minutes
Cook time 15 minutes

100 g (3½ oz/generous ½ cup) rice flour
150 ml (5 fl oz/scant ⅔ cup) coconut milk
20 g (¾ oz) soft brown sugar
½ teaspoon vanilla extract
3 ripe bananas, peeled
2–3 tablespoons coconut oil or sunflower oil

TO SERVE (OPTIONAL)

fresh fruit
ice cream

BANANA FRITTERS

BÁNH CHUỐI CHIÊN

Don't throw those browning bananas away! This is a great way to use them up and have all members of your household roar with delight. Serve with ice cream, fruit salad, homemade yoghurt (page 188) or with extra coconut cream. They are delightful eaten fresh from the pan without any extra fuss, too.

Combine the rice flour, coconut milk, sugar and vanilla extract in a large bowl, then whisk together until it is lump-free.

Slice the bananas in half lengthways and use the side of the knife to flatten the banana ever so slightly, then halve them again and add them to the batter, turning to coating each piece.

Heat half the oil in a frying pan over a medium heat, then fry the bananas in batches for 2–3 minutes on each side or until golden. Add the rest of the oil for the second or third batch. Set aside on paper towels, then serve warm as is or with fruit and ice cream, if you would like.

Serves 6–8

VIETNAMESE COFFEE TIRAMISU

TIRAMISU CÀ PHÊ

Prep time	30 minutes, plus 12 hours chilling time
Cook time	10 minutes

3 x 16 g (½ oz) sachets of instant Vietnamese coffee
300 ml (10 fl oz/1¼ cups) boiling water
3 medium egg yolks
150 ml (5 fl oz/scant ⅔ cup) condensed milk
250 g (9 oz) mascarpone
250 ml (8 fl oz/1 cup) double (heavy) cream
320 g (11¼ oz) sponge fingers
2 tablespoons cocoa (unsweetened chocolate) powder

NOTE

If you have a Vietnamese coffee maker (*phin*), make 300 ml (10 fl oz/1¼ cups) Vietnamese ground coffee, adding 100 ml (3½ fl oz/scant ½ cup) condensed milk. Stir and leave to cool.

To me and to many others, Vietnamese coffee is the best in the world. Tiramisu is also something we always order at Italian restaurants, but the Vietnamese coffee takes this much-loved dessert to another level. Save the egg whites for meringues or a pavlova.

First, make the Vietnamese coffee by pouring the instant Vietnamese coffee into a jug (pitcher) and pouring over the boiling water. Stir to dissolve.

Fill a saucepan with 2.5 cm (1 inch) water and bring to a gentle simmer. Place a large heatproof bowl over the top and add the egg yolks and condensed milk. Whisk for 5 minutes until they become pale and fluffy. Then add the mascarpone and whisk for a further 3–5 minutes until thickened and combined. Remove from the heat and set aside.

With an electric whisk, by hand or in a stand mixer, whisk the double cream for about 5 minutes until it almost reaches soft peaks, but is still soft and glossy, then fold the cream into the egg and mascarpone mixture.

Dip half the sponge fingers into the coffee for a second or two, then line them up in a 25 x 30 cm (10 x 12 inch) square cake tin (pan) or deep rectangular baking dish. Spread over half of the cream mixture, then sift over a layer of cocoa powder. Repeat with the remaining sponge fingers, cream and cocoa powder.

Refrigerate for at least 12 hours before serving.

Serves 6–8

TOFU PUDDING WITH GINGER SYRUP

TÀU HỦ NƯỚC ĐƯỜNG

Prep time 5 minutes, plus 1½ hours soaking and chilling time
Cook time 15 minutes

1 litre (34 fl oz/4¼ cups) Fresh Soya Milk (page 195)
1¼ teaspoons agar flakes
40 g (1½ oz) rock sugar

FOR THE GINGER SYRUP

500 ml (17 fl oz/generous 2 cups) water
80 g (2¾ oz) palm sugar or rock sugar
40 g (1½ oz) fresh ginger root, peeled and sliced into matchsticks

Typically Vietnamese, this bowl of goodness is a perfect balance of refreshing and warming elements. Serve as dessert after a meal to soothe and comfort in all climates.

Pour the soya milk into a saucepan. Add the agar flakes, gently stir and leave to soak for 30 minutes.

Add the rock sugar to the milk and bring to a gentle simmer. Cook for 10 minutes without stirring, then give it a gentle stir for a minute. Pour into a flat container like a baking dish or loaf pan. Let the milk cool to room temperature, then refrigerate. It will set quite quickly.

To make the ginger syrup, combine all the ingredients in a saucepan and bring to a simmer to dissolve the sugar. Simmer and infuse for at least 5 minutes. Refrigerate if you want to serve the dish cold.

To serve, scoop thin spoonfuls of the set tofu jelly into bowls and pour over the syrup. This can be enjoyed warm on colder evenings or cold during the summer.

Makes 12 muffins

HONEYCOMB, PANDAN AND COCONUT MUFFINS

BÁNH BÒ NƯỚNG

Prep time 20 minutes
Cook time 40 minutes

2 tablespoons coconut or neutral oil
285 g (10 oz/1⅔ cups) tapioca flour
2 tablespoons rice flour
2 tablespoons baking powder
pinch of sea salt
100 ml (3½ fl oz/scant ½ cup Pandan Extract (page 209, or see below)
300 ml (10 fl oz/1¼ cups) coconut milk
140 g (5 oz/scant ⅔ cup) caster (superfine) sugar
5 medium eggs

Bánh bò translates as 'climbing' or 'crawling' cake as the batter needs surfaces to cling onto as it rises, giving it a unique honeycomb texture. This recipe would also work in a bundt tins (cook for 55 minutes) as well as small cupcake tins (cook for 15 minutes). It is traditionally steamed in bamboo baskets, but I am still working out that carefully guarded secret method. These can be made with pandan or just plain coconut, and sometimes pink colouring is added to the coconut ones to make a multicoloured treat. Try it with beetroot (beet) juice instead of pandan extract, too.

Use a pastry brush to grease the holes of a 12-hole muffin tin (pan) with the 1 tablespoon of oil. Preheat the oven to 180°C fan (400°F) and place a muffin tin inside to heat up.

Combine the flours, baking powder and salt in a large bowl and mix together.

In a separate large bowl, stir together the pandan extract, coconut milk and caster sugar until there are no longer any grains. Sift the dry ingredients into the coconut milk mixture. Gently whisk together until there are no lumps.

Crack the eggs into another large mixing bowl. Using a pair of scissors or chopsticks, break the yolks into quarters. Do not mix or beat. Pour the eggs into the bowl of batter and set the bowl that had the eggs in it aside. Gently fold the eggs into the batter for a minute. There will still be lumps of egg whites and yolk – that's OK.

Place a sieve (fine mesh strainer) onto the bowl that had the eggs in it and run the batter mix through the sieve, using a spoon to pass it through. Add the remaining tablespoon of the oil to the batter and gently mix in.

Remove the muffin tin from the oven. Fill each hole to the top with the batter, then swirl a fork through the batter in the shape of the letter S.

Bake for 20 minutes on the top shelf, then leave the muffins inside the oven with the oven door ajar for a further 20 minutes.

Remove from the oven and allow to cool for at least 10 minutes before serving.

NOTES

If you don't want to make your own pandan extract, use 1 teaspoon of shop-bought pandan extract and 400 ml (14 fl oz/generous 1½ cups) coconut milk. If you can't get hold of any kind of pandan, just make them without or with vanilla extract.

Serves 4–6

SWEETCORN RICE PUDDING

CHÈ BẮP

Prep time 2 hours 5 minutes
Cook time 30 minutes

- 1 x 325 g (11½ oz) tin of sweetcorn or 2 corn cobs
- 120 g (4¼ oz/scant ⅔ cup) glutinous rice, soaked for at least 2 hours
- 35 g (1¼ oz) palm or rock sugar
- 600 ml (20 fl oz/2½ cups) coconut water or water
- 2 pandan leaves, tied into a knot (optional)
- 400 ml (14 fl oz/generous 1½ cups) coconut milk
- 20 g (9¾ oz/1 tablespoon, plus 2 teaspoons) caster (superfine) sugar
- ¼ teaspoon sea salt
- ½ tablespoon cornflour (cornstarch) mixed with 2 tablespoons water

This is such a great storecupboard dessert, which would of course be made from fresh ingredients in Vietnam. In the summer months, when corn is in season, use fresh corn and serve this cold. On colder nights, serve it warm and take comfort in the soothing texture. I've eaten this on many occasions in the markets of Vietnam. Sometimes the corn is ground and the pudding is very smooth. Here, I've gone for coarse as I prefer the crunchy texture of sweetcorn. Occasionally, market sellers don't use glutinous rice at all but lots of cornflour (cornstarch) to create a thick, sweet soup. In the northern regions, the dessert is treacly sweet, while in the south it is saltier. Either way, it is definitely a Vietnamese favourite.

Put the sweetcorn into a food processor and pulse to chop the kernels.

Transfer the sweetcorn to a saucepan and add the glutinous rice, palm or rock sugar and 400 ml (14 fl oz/generous 1½ cups) of the coconut water or water. Throw in the pandan knot, if using.

Simmer over a medium-low heat for 20 minutes until the mixture has thickened to a porridge consistency. Stir occasionally to prevent the rice from catching on the bottom of the pan.

Once thickened, add the rest of the coconut water.

Pour the coconut milk into a small saucepan and add the caster sugar and salt. Cook over a medium heat, stirring, for 2 minutes until the sugar has dissolved. Add the cornflour and water mixture and continue to simmer for a few minutes until the mixture has thickened to a custard consistency, then remove from the heat.

Serve the rice pudding with the coconut milk poured over it.

Serves 8

Prep time	20 minutes
Cook time	35 minutes

100 g (3½ oz) salted butter
70 g (2½ oz/scant ⅓ cup) caster (superfine) or brown sugar
2 medium eggs
100 g (3½ oz/generous ¾ cup) self-raising flour
1 teaspoon baking powder
4 heaped tablespoons desiccated (dried shredded) coconut
200 g (7 oz) berries and cherries, halved and stoned (or other fruits, see introduction)
1 tablespoon flaked (slivered) almonds or raw coconut chips (optional)
1 teaspoon icing (confectioners') sugar (optional)
coconut or homemade Vietnamese yoghurt (page 188) or custard and fruit salad drizzled with honey, to serve

BERRIES AND CHERRIES COCONUT CAKE

BÁNH NƯỚNG DỪA QUẢ MỌNG

I've been perfecting this cake recipe since I was a teenager, baking without recipes and hoping for a cake at the end. This simple cake recipe uses cherries and berries, but it would also work well with plums, nectarines or peaches. It is also great with tinned fruit such as peaches and pears or frozen berries. If you have any fresh Pandan Extract (page 209) going, add 2 tablespoons to the mixture.

Preheat the oven to 160°C fan (350°F). Grease a 20 cm (8 inch) springform cake tin (pan) and line with baking parchment.

Beat the butter and sugar with an electric whisk or in a stand mixer until light and fluffy, then add the eggs one at a time, beating between each addition. Once all the eggs have been added, add the flour and baking powder and mix again until smooth. Add the desiccated coconut and mix to combine.

Pour the batter into the prepared cake tin, then dot the berries and cherries onto the cake and lightly tap them down with your fingers. Scatter the flaked almonds or coconut chips over the top, if using.

Bake in the oven for 35 minutes, or until a skewer inserted into the centre comes out clean. Remove from the oven and allow to cool in the tin for at least 10 minutes. Remove from the tin and lightly dust with icing sugar, if desired.

Serve with coconut or homemade Vietnamese yoghurt or custard and a fruit salad drizzled with honey. In colder months, this is great with custard.

Makes 8 x 120 ml (4 fl oz/½ cup) jars

VIETNAMESE YOGHURT

SỮA CHUA VIETNAM

Prep time	1 minute, plus 6–10 hours setting time
Cook time	10 minutes

1 litre (34 fl oz/4¼ cups) whole milk
90 g (3¼ oz) condensed milk
2–3 tablespoons live plain yoghurt

This recipe reminds me deeply of my lovely childhood in Sài Gòn. I can hear myself scraping the jars of yoghurt clean. My cousin, Thuý, demonstrated her recipe to me years ago. Instead of jars, she would use plastic bags for the yoghurt, tying them up with an elastic band and leaving double the room for the fermentation gases. She would put a large pan into a bin bag, fill the pan with hot (not boiling) water and stand the yoghurt bags on a bamboo steamer over the water. She would then tie up the bag and let it sit for 8 hours. Admittedly the climate in Vietnam is already around 30°C (86°F), which is the perfect temperature for the yoghurt to cultivate. It was absolutely delicious! You would cut off one end of the yoghurt bags and suck the yoghurt out.

I love this on its own, without anything, but you can add fruit if you like.

Combine the milk and condensed milk in a large saucepan and bring to a simmer over a medium-low heat, stirring gently. When the mixture starts to gently steam, remove the pan from the heat, remove the skin and let it cool to about 45°C (113°F). If you don't have a thermometer, it should be lukewarm to the touch and cool enough that you don't have to blow on it before tasting it.

Mix in the plain yoghurt then pour into jars, yoghurt pots, tumblers or ramekins. Place in a warm, just used oven (below 70°C/160°F) with a mugful of hot water (two in colder months) and leave to set for 8–10 hours. The longer you leave it the more it will ferment and become sour.

Once fermented to you liking, cover and refrigerate. Consume within one week.

NOTE

Always save one jar of the yoghurt as a starter for the next batch. Instead of condensed milk, stir in honey or a fruit preserve while it is cooling. For unsweetened, leave out any source of sweetness.

Serves 6–8

COCONUT, JELLY AND FRUIT COCKTAIL BUBBLE TEA

TRÀ SỮA TRÁI CÂY

Prep time 15 minutes, plus 40 minutes soaking and setting time
Cook time 15 minutes

FOR THE JELLIES

250 ml (8 fl oz/1 cup) aloe vera juice
250 ml (8 fl oz/1 cup) coconut water
1½ teaspoons agar flakes
150 ml (5 fl oz/scant ⅔ cup
Pandan Extract (page 209, or use ½ teaspoon shop-bought)

FOR THE TEA

600 ml (20 fl oz/2½ cups) coconut water
50 g (1¾ oz) rock sugar
80 g (2¾ oz) large, fast cooking tapioca pearls
2 tablespoons small tapioca pearls
300 ml (10 fl oz/1¼ cups) coconut milk (high coconut percentage)

FOR THE FRUIT COCKTAIL

1 mango, peeled and diced
1 x 565 g (20 oz) tin of longans, lychees or rambutans, drained and halved
100 g (3½ oz) raspberries or pomegranate seeds (optional)
500 g (1 lb 2 oz) coconut flesh (optional)

NOTE

If fresh longans, rambutans and lychees are available, use those. Add as many exotic fruits as you desire. If there is no time to make jelly, shop-bought tins of grass jelly in black and green are very tasty.

Make sure to buy 5-minute cooking time tapioca pearls (it clearly states it on the packaging), as otherwise they need soaking and cooking for over 30 minutes.

This is a great dessert to serve after a feast, as it can be made in advance and left in a punch bowl for everyone to serve themselves. Or, it can be a lovely and simple thing to make using as much or as little of whatever you have around. I love making agar jelly because it sets really quickly. I get this going first and then get on with creating a whole meal. By the end, the jelly is ready to add to the tea. If you want to add matcha powder to the tea, use 1 teaspoon of matcha powder mixed with 1 tablespoon of water. Feel free to mix and match with fresh ingredients and whatever you have in the pantry. Sometimes I use just mango, or I add bananas in with the tapioca.

To make the jellies, pour the aloe vera juice into a small saucepan and pour the coconut water into a separate small saucepan. Divide the agar flakes between the two and set aside to soak for 30 minutes.

Bring both pans to a gentle boil without stirring, then stir the mixture and cook for 5 minutes. Add the pandan extract to the coconut mixture and stir in. Pour the jelly mixtures into separate deep dishes. Let the jellies cool to room temperature, then transfer to the refrigerator. The great thing about agar is that it should set within 10 minutes of being in the refrigerator. Once set, slice into cubes.

To make the milk tea, pour the coconut water into a saucepan and add the rock sugar. Bring to a simmer, then add the large tapioca pearls. Simmer for about 5 minutes, then add the smaller pearls. Cook for a further 5 minutes, then add the coconut milk, bring to the boil, then remove from the heat and leave to cool to room temperature before chilling in the refrigerator for up to 2 hours (after this point the tapioca pearls will stiffen).

To serve, put the fruits and jelly cubes into bowls or glasses, add ice (if using), and ladle over the tea.

ARTICHOKE TEA

TRÀ ARTISO

Serves 4–6

Prep time 10 minutes
Cook time 20 minutes

4 globe artichokes (pick ones that are heavy and squeaky)
juice of ½ lemon
20 g (¾ oz) rock sugar (optional)

Refreshing and healthy, this can be served hot or cold throughout the day or with meals.

Slice the top off the artichokes (about a third of the artichoke) with a serrated knife. Cut off the excess stem and remove any small leaves by the stem. Rinse and open up the leaves and then place the artichokes in a large saucepan. Submerge the artichokes in about 2 litres (68 fl oz/8½ cups) of water and the lemon juice and rock sugar, if using. Weigh down the artichokes with a clean plate. Bring to a simmer and gently cook for 20 minutes. Remove the artichokes from the broth with tongs and set aside.

Serve the tea hot or cool to room temperature before chilling in the refrigerator.

NOTE

You can add the artichoke hearts to a salad or noodles after cooking. To prepare them, cut the artichoke into quarters, remove the furry 'chokes' with a teaspoon and rub the hearts with rapeseed (canola) oil. Heat a griddle pan and char the artichoke hearts, flat side down. Set aside to cool to room temperature before using.

BASIL SEED DRINK

NƯỚC HỘT É

Serves 2

Prep time 1 minute

1 tablespoon basil seeds
300 ml (10 fl oz/1¼ cups) cold artichoke tea
honey, to taste (optional)

This is a cooling and healthy drink consumed all over Vietnam.

Mix the basil seeds and cold artichoke tea together. Watch the seeds develop a white opaque coating, then stir in a little honey, if desired.

Serves 4

FRESH SOYA MILK

SỮA ĐẬU NÀNH

Prep time	10 minutes, plus 6 hours soaking time
Cook time	30 minutes

100 g (3½ oz/1⅔ cups) high-quality dried soya beans
1 litre (34 fl oz/4¼ cups) water
15 g (½ oz) rock sugar (optional)

Making your own soya milk is really easy. Its knowing that it has not been processed in a factory that sells it to me. Soya milk is consumed on a regular basis in Vietnam – a hot one for breakfast and cooling ones throughout the day. Hailed for its many health benefits and protein levels, I love it in my tea as well and make extra for Tofu & Ginger dessert.

Put the soya beans into a bowl and cover with boiling water. Set aside to soak for 6 hours, or overnight.

The next day, drain and wash the beans. Transfer to a food processor with the 1 litre (34 fl oz/4¼ cups) water and blend until it is smooth and silky.

Line a sieve (fine mesh strainer) with muslin (cheesecloth) and place it over a bowl. Pour the blended beans into the sieve and squeeze out the milk. You should be left with a dry pulp, which you can compost.

Pour the milk into a saucepan and bring to a simmering boil – watch it closely because it may suddenly boil over. Once it starts to boil, reduce the heat to low and skim off any foam or residue. Add the rock sugar, if using, then cover and cook for 20 minutes. Do not skip the cooking as soya beans need to be cooked before consumption – they are considered poisonous when raw.

Serve warm or chill in the refrigerator and use within 3 days.

8 BASICS

BASICS

'We are a fussy-eater family,' laughed my sister-in-law, My, who entered a family in which no one is afraid to give an opinion or two about how things should be done. 'If the rice is not cooked perfectly, no one will eat it and everyone complains.' Even at age five, my daughter Olive – who loves eating good food – will only eat perfectly fluffy rice, al dente spaghetti and noodles and dishes with well-balanced seasoning.

I will always choose my mum's cooking whenever I can – her kitchen is the best restaurant in the world. I have always been amazed at how quick and easy her Vietnamese cooking is. The prep is the main work, and the devil is often in the details. Using the right ingredients, such as crystals of Maldon sea salt, Three Crabs or Red Boat fish sauce and red bird's eye chillies makes a huge difference to the overall result.

Getting to know the basics like cooking (not boiling!) rice and rehydrating noodles is an essential life skill.

Getting to know the capabilities of pots and pans and which to use for what recipe is a good idea, too. Make broth in a suitable stockpot, fry egg fried rice in a wok or large frying pan, make sauces in a small milk pan and so on. Become familiar with the strengths and flavours of storecupboard ingredients, as well. Figure out how sweet or salty particular brands are. When it comes to vegetables, eat all the colours of the seasons and enjoy them at their best.

As we do tend to be time-poor, there is nothing wrong with using stock cubes or buying yoghurt, kimchi and noodles, but sometimes homemade is best.

I often think to myself that I hope to become like my grandmothers, surrounded by baskets of herbs in my kitchen, with broth bubbling away among the mountains of noodles draining in colanders and artful dumplings being steamed and a pandan cake rising in the oven. Sometimes I am the embodiment of them, but sometimes I cheat.

Serves 4

300 g (10½ oz/scant 1¾ cups) jasmine rice
500 ml (17 fl oz/generous 2 cups) water

PLAIN RICE

CƠM TRẮNG

Steamed rice is a staple and it is important to cook it well because it is a vessel that carries many recipes. If you enjoy rice and Vietnamese food, invest in a simple rice cooker to give ease into everyday meals. It is the most used appliance in any Vietnamese household.

To cook rice, there is no better way to do it than in a basic rice cooker. When the rice is cooked, fluff it up with a wooden or plastic paddle or spatula, by mixing and turning it around, then leave the rice to rest and fluff up in the cooker for a further 5–10 minutes.

If you don't have a rice cooker, cook the rice with the water in a saucepan with a lid over a medium-low heat. After 5 minutes, when the water has seeped into the rice and there isn't any water on the surface, turn the heat down to low and cook with the lid securely on to let the steam do its work for a further 15–18 minutes. Then turn off the heat without removing the lid and let it rest for 5–10 minutes, before fluffing up the rice with a rice paddle or wooden spoon. (You will often get a crispy or burnt bottom this way, which is a treat in itself.) The aim is to get fluffy, cooked-just-right rice that isn't sticking together in clumps, too soft and watery or hard and chalky. Your rice is perfect when you can sink your teeth into it and it has a lovely, mild nutty and floral flavour.

Serves 4

STICKY RICE WITH RED BEANS

XÔI ĐẬU ĐỎ

Prep time 2 hours 10 minutes
Cook time 55 minutes

- 200 g (7 oz/1 cup) glutinous rice, soaked for at least 2 hours or overnight
- ½ tablespoon rapeseed (canola) oil
- 1 garlic clove, sliced
- 100 g (3½ oz) tinned adzuki beans, drained and rinsed
- ¼ teaspoon caster (superfine) sugar
- ¼ teaspoon sea salt
- 1 teaspoon light soy sauce
- 1 spring onion (scallions), sliced
- Crispy Shallots (page 208; optional)

Sticky rice is usually served on special occasions or when you have guests coming for dinner. Its luxurious, velvety texture is so satisfying. It's also common to add other grains or seeds to the mix, like mung beans, peanuts and haricot (navy) beans. Sometimes the rice is also perfumed with a knot of pandan leaf or coloured red with sweet gourd (*xôi gấc*) to bring luck, prosperity and a wonderful flavour. So much can be done to dress sticky rice, even simply cooking it with coconut milk and sprinkling with desiccated (dried shredded) coconut adds to its character.

Line a steamer basket with a liner or with baking parchment with some holes punched into it. Spread the glutinous rice out in the steamer and steam over a low heat for 45 minutes until the rice is soft. If the grains have been soaking overnight, the steaming time may be shorter.

Meanwhile, heat the oil in a frying pan over a medium heat and fry the garlic for 1 minute until golden. Add the adzuki beans, sugar, salt and soy sauce. Stir-fry for 5 minutes, then remove from the heat.

When the rice is cooked, fold through the beans and shower with the spring onion and crispy shallots, if using. Serve hot or at room temperature.

Serves as many as you like

EGG FRIED RICE

CƠM CHIÊN TRỨNG

Prep time 5 minutes
Cook time 10 minutes

- a little ghee or rapeseed (canola) oil
- 1–2 garlic cloves, finely chopped or roughly sliced
- yesterday's leftover cold rice
- soy sauce or mushroom seasoning powder (or a little of both)
- spring onions (scallions), sliced
- freshly ground black pepper
- 1–2 eggs (any size)

OPTIONAL ADDITIONS

- vegetables and herbs, such as peas, sweetcorn, carrot, edamame, mushrooms, coriander (cilantro), chives or whatever you have left over
- pickles and storecupboard ingredients, such as pickled mustard greens, kimchi, crispy shallots, curry powder

As a home comfort by itself or to dress up rice meals and feasts, egg fried rice is simple and special. It is as good as what you give it, but knowing when not to overdo it is key too. Don't overload it. I like to use a little sprinkling of mushroom seasoning powder because it delivers a good punch of umami while not colouring the rice too much. Using cold leftover rice is ideal for this, and, since you never know how much leftovers there will be, I haven't included exact measurements here. Go with your common sense. Freshly cooked rice is OK but it tends to get mushy in the pan so let it go to room temperature before use. I like to enjoy my bowl with a fried egg on top and lots of Maggi seasoning.

Heat the ghee or oil in a wok over a medium-high heat and add the garlic and any frozen vegetables, if using. As soon as the garlic starts to colour, add the rice, soy sauce or mushroom seasoning powder, spring onions and black pepper. Fold it all in together, then make a well in the centre of the wok. Crack in the eggs and let it sit for 30 seconds, then scramble the egg briefly. Let it cook 30 seconds longer, then combine with the rice. Add any cooked vegetables, if using, and vigorously stir-fry until everything is well combined and hot. Add any herbs or pickles and toss through.

Makes 8–9 buns

BAO BUNS

BÁNH BAO

Prep time 30 minutes, plus 50 minutes resting time
Cook time 10 minutes

- 250 g (9 oz/2 cups) strong white bread flour, plus extra for dusting
- 4 g (1½ teaspoons) fast-action dried yeast
- 3 tablespoons caster (superfine) sugar
- ½ tablespoon sea salt, finely crushed
- 4 g (1 teaspoon) baking powder
- 75 ml (2½ fl oz/5 tablespoons) whole milk
- 75 ml (2½ fl oz/5 tablespoons) water, plus extra as needed

FILLING OPTIONS

Char Sui Pork Belly (page 154)
Dill Fishcakes (page 136)
Steamed Egg Terrine (page 141)
Roast Plum and Clementine Duck (page 141)
Bánh Hoi Platter and Summer Roll Party (page 146)

These bao buns are the open sandwich type that can be filled and stuffed.

Cut out eight 10 cm (4 inch) squares of baking parchment and set aside.

Pour the flour into the bowl of a stand mixer fitted with the dough hook attachment and make a well in the centre. Add the yeast and sugar. Sprinkle the salt and baking powder around the edge of bowl on top of the flour.

Depending on the brand of flour you use, the amount of liquid you will need will vary. Pour the milk into the well and slowly combine, then add enough water to bring it together into a dough. Knead with the dough hook for approximately 5 minutes until the dough forms a smooth, clean ball.

Roll out the dough into a sausage about 30 cm (12 inches) long, then divide in half and divide each half into four pieces. Each piece should weigh about 50 g (1¾ oz). Put the pieces of dough into an airtight container to rest while you work.

Roll out one of the dough balls into a circle about 15 cm (6 inches) in diameter on a lightly dusted surface. Use a chopstick to make an indentation across the middle of the circle, then fold it in half to make a half-moon shape. Place on one of the sheets of baking parchment and transfer to a steamer basket.

Repeat with the rest of the dough. Place the baskets or tray of buns inside a cold oven with a mugful of boiling water in the bottom and leave to rise for about 50 minutes until doubled in size.

Meanwhile, cover the inside of the steamer lid with a dish towel and tie the ends together on the outside. Bring a steamer pan or half-filled saucepan of water to the boil and place a basket of bao buns on top, making sure the water does not touch the steamer basket itself. Cover and steam for 6–8 minutes until doubled in size, puffed up and springy to the touch. When they are cooked, remove from the heat and leave the lid ajar for 2–3 minutes.

NOTES

Make sure you have sliced cucumbers, spring onions (scallions), mint or coriander (cilantro) and some pickles to finish them with for a perfect balance of flavours and textures.

Makes about 2 litres (68 fl oz/8½ cups)

Prep time 1 hour, plus 2–3 days fermenting time

- 2½ tablespoons sea salt
- 1.6 litres (54 fl oz/6¾ cups) water
- 600 g (1 lb 5 oz) Chinese (napa) cabbage, cored, cut into 5 cm (2 inch) pieces and washed thoroughly
- 4 small round shallots, sliced
- 4 spring onions (scallions), sliced lengthways
- 100 g (3½ oz) carrot, cut into long matchsticks
- 1 apple or Asian pear, cut into 1 cm (½ inch) cubes
- 150 g (5½ oz) daikon, cut into long matchsticks
- 1 red chilli, finely chopped

FOR THE PASTE

- 40 g (1½ oz) fresh ginger root, peeled
- 30 g (1 oz) garlic cloves, peeled
- 2 tablespoons fish sauce
- 2½ tablespoons white wine, cider or rice vinegar
- 50 g (1¾ oz) Korean red pepper flakes (gochugaru)
- 40 g (1½ oz/scant ¼ cup) soft brown sugar
- 1½ teaspoons sea salt

NOTES

This is a great vessel to add other vegetables, such as cauliflower, radish, beetroot (beets), etc.

EASY KIMCHI

KIM CHI

At the Vietnamese table, ferments are used daily to incorporate a sour element into dishes but also to bring goodness into our diet. Food scientist Tim Spector outlines in his book, *Food for Life*, how ferments like kimchi are essential for our gut health. I always used to buy a weekly supply of kimchi in a packet or plastic jar, but after reading Su Scott's wonderful book, *Rice Table*, I was inspired to create my own recipe, combining many of her kimchi techniques. It doesn't have to be as labour intensive as you might think and every jar will taste different. It is as if the way you handle the vegetables has a great effect on the final outcome. Treated with care and attention, you do reap what you sow.

Put the salt and water into a large bowl, then add the washed cabbage leaves and submerge them, weighing them down with a heavy plate if necessary. Leave to stand for 1 hour, stirring halfway through.

Drain the cabbage thoroughly (without rinsing) and add the other vegetables to the bowl.

Put all the ingredients for the paste into a food processor and blend until smooth. Using tongs or gloved hands, gently massage the paste into the vegetables until well combined. Bruising the vegetables a little helps with the fermentation process.

Sterilise a large jar by running it through a hot dishwasher cycle or boiling it for 3 minutes before leaving to air dry, then fill it with the kimchi mixture. Wipe down with a clean paper towel if necessary, then leave to ferment at room temperature away from direct sunlight for 2–5 days until the vegetables have wilted and the juices are bubbling. Flick the lid open every day to 'burp' the jar and release any built-up gases. After this time, transfer to the refrigerator. It will keep for about 1 month. Transfer to smaller jars for gifts.

CRISPY SHALLOTS

HÀNH PHI

Makes approx. 300 g (10 oz)

Prep time 15 minutes
Cook time 15 minutes

4 tablespoons vegetable oil
12 round shallots, thinly sliced

These are used as toppings to elevate any dish, but they also flavour broths remarkably well.

Heat the oil in a frying pan (skillet) over a low heat and fry the shallot until golden, then remove from the heat. Drain in a sieve (fine mesh strainer) reserving the excess flavoured oil. Drain on paper towels. They will continue to brown and crisp. Save the shallot oil and crispy shallots in two separate containers for future use with noodle soups and to garnish rice, noodles and salads.

SPRING ONION OIL

Makes 1 portion

Prep time 5 minutes
Cook time 3–5 minutes

1 spring onion (scallion) per person
1 tablespoon per person extra virgin olive oil
pinch of sea salt

Cook the spring onions in the olive oil in a small saucepan over a low heat with a pinch of salt for a couple of minutes until the spring onions have wilted.

Makes 200 ml
(7 fl oz/scant 1 cup)

PANDAN EXTRACT

NƯỚC LÁ DỨA

Prep time 5 minutes

50 g (1¾ oz) fresh pandan leaves, washed, trimmed and cut into 10 cm (4 inch) lengths
200 ml (7 oz) water

The smell of pandan is the essence of home to me. I love its perfume and delicious grassy flavour in desserts. You can add as little or as much water to the extract as you like depending on how far you want to stretch it and how intense you want the flavour to be. It's great in desserts and rice porridge.

Combine the pandan leaves and water in a food processor and blend until the leaves are finely processed, then pass through a fine sieve (fine mesh strainer) into a bowl. Squeeze out all the juices from the leaves with your hands and discard (or place in a fine muslin/cheesecloth or tea strainer and make a pot of tea).

Use immediately or store in a clean glass jar in the refrigerator for up to a week. The pandan will naturally separate and sink to the bottom of the jar – if you want to, you can pour out some of the water for a more intense extract.

Serves 2

VERMICELLI NOODLE SALAD BOWLS

BÚN

Prep time 25 minutes
Cook time 5 minutes

160 g (5½ oz) 0.8 mm rice vermicelli
2 tablespoons vegetable oil
2 spring onions (scallions), sliced
a handful of anything green and leafy, such as lamb's lettuce, watercress, rocket (arugula) or lettuce
a handful of Vietnamese herbs, such as coriander (cilantro), mint and Thai basil
spring onion oil (page 208)
2 heaped tablespoons peanuts, pistachios or cashews, finely chopped
pickles or ferments of your choice, such as kimchi (shop-bought or homemade, page 207), pickled carrots or gherkins (pickles)

FOR THE DRESSING

½ bird's eye chilli, finely chopped
1 tablespoon honey or caster (superfine) sugar
1 tablespoon premium fish sauce, shop-bought perilla dressing or light soy sauce
finely chopped zest and juice of ½ lime or ¼ lemon
2 tablespoons hot water

TOPPINGS

Prawn, Sweet Potato and Courgette Fritters (page 160)
Char Siu Crispy Pork Belly (page 154) (pictured)
Haddock Spring Rolls (page 163)
Plummy Aubergines (page 66)
King Prawn and Mango Rice Paper Salad (page 210)
Sweet and Sour Crispy Tofu with Green Beans (page 65)
Steamed Egg Terrine (page 141)
Dill Fishcakes (page 136)
Sliced Pork Chop with Kimchi and Lemongrass (page 126)
Lemongrass Meat Skewers (page 102) (pictured)

For a complete bowl of goodness and immense pleasure with plenty of flavours and textures from plants, make this. It can be the base for so many different toppings. Enjoy with pickles and ferments and add as much or as little variety of leaves and herbs as you like. The more fragrant the herbs, the better.

Put the noodles into a large bowl and cover with boiling water, then leave to soak for 5–10 minutes (check the packet instructions). Drain, then rinse under warm water. Cover and set aside to dry and fluff up for 10–15 minutes.

Make the dressing by combining all the ingredients in a jar and shaking well.

To assemble, place the greens and herbs into shallow bowls, then add the noodles on one side and smother with the spring onion oil. Spoon the nuts into a corner and the pickles or ferments into another corner. Top with one of the suggested toppings, then pour over the dressing and serve immediately.

Serves 4–5

Prep time	40 minutes, plus 20 minutes resting time
Cook time	5–8 minutes

200 g (7 oz) frozen spinach, defrosted
500 g (1 lb 2 oz/4 cups) 00 flour, plus extra for dusting
2 large eggs
2 tablespoons olive oil

NOTE

Use leftover herbs or other green leaves if you do not have spinach.

Feel free to omit the spinach and use 1 egg per 100 g (3½ oz/generous ¾ cup) of flour (without olive oil).

HOMEMADE SPINACH NOODLES

MÌ CẢI BÓ XÔI

There is nothing better than making your own noodles, and these are an absolute winner that can be used in so many ways.

Put the spinach into a food processor and blend until smooth, then set aside to rest for 5 minutes. Squeeze out the water.

You can make the dough either in a stand mixer or by hand.

If using a stand mixer, put the all the ingredients into the bowl of the mixer (including the spinach purée) and knead with the dough hook for about 8 minutes until the dough is smooth, adding a little more flour if it looks wet.

If making by hand, put the flour onto a clean work surface, make a well in the centre and crack the eggs in. Pour in the oil, then use a fork to beat the eggs. Add the spinach and combine everything with the flour. Use a dough scraper to bring the dough together, then knead by hand for 10–12 minutes until the dough is smooth and bounces back when you tap it.

Cover the dough and leave to rest for at least 20 minutes, then divide it into eight equal-sized pieces. Keep the pieces in a lidded container or cover with a dish towel as you work.

Flatten and dust each piece of dough with flour, then feed through a pasta machine set to level 1 until the sheet becomes smooth, about 6–8 times. Keep dusting with flour when necessary and then feed through the machine until you reach level 5. Lay each sheet on a lightly floured surface while you repeat with the rest of the dough.

Cut the pasta by hand with a knife at similar widths or run through a tagliatelle cutter. Bring together into a loose ball, then cover and leave to dry on a lightly floured surface, turning every few hours until dry.

To cook, bring a large saucepan of salted water to the boil and cook the noodles for 5–8 minutes until al dente.

Serves 2

HOMEMADE THICK-CUT NOODLES

BÁNH CANH

Prep time 15 minutes
Cook time 10 minutes

125 g (4½ oz/scant ¾ cup) tapioca flour, plus extra for dusting
100 g (3½ oz/generous ½ cup) rice flour
175 ml (6 fl oz/¾ cup) boiling water
neutral oil, for drizzling

These crowd-pleasing noodles are great in a stir-fry for a super-speedy, cook-from-scratch dinner. They are also wonderful in noodle soups. They are so quick and easy and you will impress everyone with their toothsome deliciousness and comforting flavour.

Combine the two flours in a large bowl.

Clean and dry a large cutting board and dust with flour. Get a rolling pin, a pizza cutter or knife, a spatula and a measuring jug or cup ready. Bring some water to the boil in a kettle.

As soon as the kettle has boiled, quickly measure out the water and pour it in a circular motion into the flours. Using a spatula, quickly bring the dough together. It will be soft and flaky. After a minute, tip the dough out onto the floured board. Use your hands to knead the dough together into a smooth, playdough-like consistency. If it feels stiff and dry add another teaspoon or two of hot water. Continue to knead for a couple of minutes, then use a rolling pin to roll out the dough to 3 mm (⅛ in) thick. Use a knife or pizza cutter to cut it into 3 mm (⅛ in) thick strips. Dust with a little more flour.

To cook, bring a large saucepan of water to the boil and add the noodles. Cook for a minute, then use chopsticks to separate the noodles and stop them from sticking to the bottom of the pan. Simmer for 5 minutes if using in a noodle soup or 3 minutes if frying (taste them to see if you would like to cook them for a couple of minutes more – they should be soft but still with some bite to them). Drain and rinse under hot water, then add a drizzle of oil and toss to prevent them from sticking together.

The noodles keep well for up to 5 days in the refrigerator.

NOTE

Once you have formed the dough, it can be refrigerated for up to 5 days for later use.

NOODLES

To really enjoy Vietnamese, it is very important to cook your noodles right. Good texture is everything. Perfectly cooked noodles are dry and fluffy with length intact. Different dishes require different sized and shaped noodles.

Rice vermicelli & flat rice noodles

Make sure you buy 0.8 mm rice vermicelli, which tend to suit most recipes. To rehydrate rice vermicelli and flat noodles, simply add to a bowl, cover with boiling kettle water for approximately 4–10 minutes depending on type and brand then drain and rinse with hot tap water until the water run clear. Leave in a covered colander to dry off and fluff up.

Fresh egg noodle

For homemade or shop-bought fresh egg noodles, always unpack, separate and air dry them on a tray, turning over every now and again. This gives bite to the noodles. Just drench in boiling water for a couple of minutes and these could be used to fry or cook for a few minutes further for broths.

Bánh Hỏi Noodles

To prepare the sheets of noodles, place them in a large bowl and cover with boiling water. Set a timer for 1 minute 20 seconds. Drain immediately, shaking off any excess water, then leave to steam and fluff up. Place them flat on platters and smother them with the spring onion oil (see page 208).

HOW TO MAKE THE BEST SAUCES, SIMPLY

There are lots of sauces in many recipes of this book. They are a guide to a good balance of sweet, salty, sour, umami and bitter flavours, together creating a beautiful burst of flavour that is ever so satisfying to our palates.

HOW TO MAKE A DIPPING SAUCE

To simply create your own sauces at home pair opposite flavours with each other, use something salty and savoury like fish sauce or soy sauce with something sweet like sugar or maple syrup/honey... even a fruit purée or perhaps a little bit of juice or soft drinks you may have lying around and need using up.

Add the all important sour element with lemons or limes – this adds so much freshness to everything but vinegars are also wonderful, especially if you can invest in good-quality ones, and even better if they can be homemade and less industrialised ones.

Bitter flavours are also really important, you can't miss that out. This is where garlic or shallots come in and use lemon or lime zest, don't throw that out, invest in a little zest peeler or Microplane zester. The bitterness here is entwined with its fresh fragrance and flavours, giving your sauce so much more depth. But don't forget to add this at the last minute, don't cook it down and don't leave it in the sauce for ages because it will over bitter matters.

Toasted sesame seeds are a great addition for crunch, as well as extra plant intake. Texture is also important in certain dishes. Adding crushed nuts to a sauce thickens it in a coleslaw-type salad and makes it less drippy without adding any oils. However, oils can be great for a simple leafy salad because it will help cling onto the surfaces of leaves.

I love using the stems of coriander (cilantro) or some additional chopped herbs in sauces because of its freshness and flavour. If you have dehydrated any herbs, crush them into the sauce too. I like making sugared dried herbs and using these instead of any other sweet element. Killing two birds...

When a sauce asks for cooking, the process helps to combine all the flavours together. If you do not have ingredient, use a similar one that suits the flavour profile.

DURING COOKING...

In a recipe, it is faster to combine all the sauces together at the start, instead of opening and closing bottles and jars as you go. This way, the correct time can be spent cooking and you don't get flustered.

ABOUT THE AUTHOR

Uyen Luu is a writer and photographer. At the weekends, she runs her Vietnamese supper club and cooking classes, cooked by her and her family. She lives in North London with her family.

Web	www.uyenluu.com
Instagram	@loveleluu
Substack	uyenluu.substack.com

ACKNOWLEDGEMENTS

Thank you to my editor, Eila Purvis, for her constant patience, letting me extend deadlines, always smiling and enjoying all the shoot food. Endless thanks to Ruth Tewkesbury and Rebecca Knight for the publicity and marketing, and Kajal Mistry for commissioning the third in the series of Vietnamese.

I love the shooting period. It is full of repeated radio music, food and laughter. Thank you to Food Stylist, Lucy Turnball, for cooking all my recipes with the utmost care, always re-reading all the recipes and making them look so natural and beautiful. Even my mum thinks all the Vietnamese food she cooks and presents is wonderful. Thank you, Lucy! Thank you to her assistants, Immy Mucklow and Freya Matchett, for being so prepared, so intrigued and for eating up all the time. Thanks always to Laurie Noble for assisting and being Laurie, and Hannah Wilkinson for all the lovely props.

Thanks to Lucy Kingett for the work in editing. I really enjoyed the process we went through as Lucy is ever so thorough and asks me things that I need to think about in my wording and descriptions so that the recipes are easy to understand. She reads as if she is cooking – such a skill!

My heartfelt thanks to Tamara Mann, whom I met through the Jamie Oliver Cookbook Club. She lives in Switzerland and I have unfortunately never met her but she cooked most of these recipes and every day or so she would send me an update on a recipe she cooked the night before and notes any errors or opinions. Mostly she would say, 'this is sooooo good! I am definitely making this again!'. I love to see how much she has learnt about Vietnamese cooking through helping test the recipe for this book.

Thank you to my friends, old, past and new who let me feed them. Thank you to my cousins, Thuý and Thảo, for showing me what it is like to have sisters, even though afar, we are so close, our love unconditional.

Thank you to my family, my beautiful mum – her wise kindness, her endless and deepest love; for still comforting me like a child when I am unwell and for all her encouragement and most delicious cooking; my brother, who always wants to cook us lunch, and My and Benji for all the smiles and love and laughter. Thank you to James (love you), for all his love and support, enabling me to work, write books and shoot pictures, and for being the best father to Olive and taking such good care of our home and family. Thank you to our beloved dog Berry for eating all the safe leftover vegetables, ends of the rice cooker, waiting on a piece of bread and butter and licking up all the yoghurt pots.

Thank you to my beautiful daughter Olive, for teaching me the incredible power of love, compassion and joy. If these things were a blanket, they would wrap my heart up so cosy like when we sit together and enjoy an array of desserts together. Thank you for choosing me to be your mum and for teaching me how to be a good mum and a better person every day. Thank you for letting me feed you. I love you so much.

H

K

L

M

N

O

P

Q

R